The Hampshire Collection

SOUTHAMPTON CITY COUNCIL

Class number H/Gos.h

Title number 185455005S

This book is due for return on or before the last date shown
above; it may, subject to the book not being reserved by
another reader, be renewed by personal application, post, or
telephone, quoting this date and details of the book.

HAMPSHIRE COUNTY LIBRARY

THE
STORY
OF
GOSPORT

By
LEONARD WHITE, PH.D., B.Sc.

NEW REVISED EDITION

Edited by
LESLEY BURTON AND BRIAN MUSSELWHITE

The Geology of Gosport by G. R. J. BROWNING

Ensign
PUBLICATIONS

EDITORS ACKNOWLEDGEMENTS

We thank the staffs of Portsmouth Central Library, Gosport Library, Gosport Museum; the Directorate of Technical Services of the Borough of Gosport, especially Maxine Bodell, David Otley and Peter Watson; Alan Mellor of the Chief Executive's Department, Borough of Gosport; G. R. J. Browning, Consultant Geologist and Chartered Engineer; Adrian Knight, L.D.S.; Richard Martin; and Keith Dingle for his photographic work. The editors would particularly like to express their appreciation for the encouragement and assistance given by Mrs. Hilda Stenson, sister of the late Dr. L. F. W. White, Ph.D., C.B.E.

Contents

INTRODUCTION

Gosport has a proud maritime heritage and this is reflected in our magnificent harbour setting with its rich array of boats, in the important naval and military establishments and in the land and sea forts, benign now but once so threatening to foreign invaders. However, despite the pre-eminence of the Navy, Gosport today is still in essence the 'little village of Fisschar men' as the Tudor historian John Leland described it when he passed through Gosport over four hundred years ago. Even with a population approaching 80,000 the town still manages to preserve something of a village atmosphere and its citizens have retained to this day what Dr. White engagingly described as their 'fierce local patriotism'.

It is almost a quarter of a century since The Story of Gosport was first published. In that time a generation has grown up to inherit a Borough of a somewhat different complexion to that of 1964. Undoubtedly two of the happier developments since then have been the establishment of the Gosport Museum and the opening of the new Central Library. Both these institutions have been remarkably successful in stimulating interest in the town's rich history as well as encouraging research in this field. The story of Gosport had much the same effect when it first appeared and it continues to inspire local historians of all ages. In this new, revised edition of The Story of Gosport we are proud to be able to build upon Dr. White's splendid historical foundations and we hope that a new readership will share our enthusiasm. And now, as they say, read on . . .

THE EDITORS
March, 1989

CHAPTER 1

Rowner, Alverstoke and Gosport in the Middle Ages. 1096-1485

ROWNER

In 1945 the northern part of Gosport stretching from the Grange airfield to the Fareham boundary included the ancient parish of Rowner with its quaint Early English Church and a number of farms with farm houses, barns, and labourers' cottages. A few houses were beginning to spring up on the ribbon of road from Gosport to Fareham and a few of the farms had extensive areas of glasshouses. Today there is a vast housing estate (or series of estates) with a population mounting towards 20,000. In 1945 the population was negligible, now one in five of the inhabitants of Gosport reside there.

This post war estate stands upon an ancient site of which the parish church is almost (but not quite) the last reminder. The other records of antiquity, the thatched farm houses and barns, are fast disappearing. The church dates back to the late 13th century and there is evidence of earlier construction. When a thorough survey and reconstruction took place in 1873 a Norman archway was discovered over the door of the south porch. It now stands over the doorway to the vestry. The piers and arches are of the 13th century. In the north wall is a small basin and opposite to it on the south wall is a seat cut into the wall. Between the chancel and the vestry is a round arch. All these are of 13th century construction. The font probably is dated about 1400 A.D. There is an elaborate tomb of Sir John Brune dated 1559. The parish registers begin in 1590.

The immediate precincts of the church have been preserved so well that one is carried at once into the rural community of which it was so long the centre. The records of Rowner have been preserved largely because generations of the same family have been associated with the life of the parish since 1277. Rowner is recorded in the Domesday Book 1086 and also in the Anglo-Saxon Chronicle for 1114.

Domesday Book records that 'William Maldwith holds Rugenor (or Ruenore) and Coleman held it of King Edward. It was then and is now assessed at three hides. There are three ploughlands, one in demesne and five villeins and four borderers, with two ploughlands and two acres of meadow. Its value was in the time of King Edward 50/-, afterwards 60/- and now the same but pays 100/-'. The whole area was reputed to be a rich oak forest. William Maldwith lived in the Tichefield Hundred. The record shows a small village community of about a dozen families eking out a precarious living from the poor soil.

There are two views as to the way in which Rowner got its name. The word Rugenore (as used by the Anglo-Saxon Chronicle) comes from 'ruh' and 'ore' rough coast or area. This would fit in well with the wild blustery area scant two miles from the coast at what is now Browndown. Another view, however, is that the name comes from the island of Rugen on the Baltic coast and dates back to the original settlement of the Jutes who brought with them memories of their homeland. But although Jutish tribes settled in this area no evidence of their occupation of Rowner has been found.

The record in the Anglo-Saxon Chronicle stated that Henry I was at Rowner on the 15th September, 1114. It was probably from here that, at the request of the Archbishop of Canterbury, he sent a deputation consisting of the Abbot of Peterborough, John (the Archbishop's nephew) and a monk named Warren to receive from the hands of the Pope in Rome, the Archbishop's pall. The same day the King rode on to Portsmouth and took ship there.

There was an ancient legend of a connection between Rowner and the celebrated stone quarries at Binstead on the Isle of Wight. It was asserted that some of the stone destined for the rebuilding of Winchester Cathedral was used at Rowner during the period 1079-1093. It was claimed that the stone was shipped across the Solent to the nearest point at Hillhead—that more stone was unloaded than was required for Winchester and that some was used to build Rowner Church.

But we are on stronger ground in establishing a link between Rowner and the famous Cistercian Abbey at Quarr on the island. Quarr Abbey was established in 1133 and there are four original deeds recording the grant of land and other property rights to the monks at Quarr. The grants include farm buildings, a windmill and the use of a ferry boat—but there is nothing to show that a monastery was established at Rowner.

The grants are particularly valuable as an indication of the conditions of the period and the importance attached to the rights of using the mill.

1. Charter of Hamo. Brito de Leya to the Abbey of St. Mary of the Stone Quarries.

'Hamo Brito de Leya sends greetings—Know that I for the salvation of my soul and of Juliana my wife have given and in this my Charter have confirmed to the Lord and Abbey of St. Mary at Quarr as a

6

perpetual and pure alms a certain part of my land at Cherc (Chark). And I have also granted that the monks of Quarr have their ship free of toll and quietly along all that seaboard which belongs either to Cherc or to Leya'.

2.   Grant of Gilbert le Bret to the Abbey of St. Mary in the Stone Quary.

'To all the faithful of Christ who will inspect or hear of this Charter.

Gilbert le Brun of Cherc sends greetings in the Lord. Let all men know that for the salvation of my soul and of all my ancestors and heirs, I have granted and conceded in this my present charter to God and the Blessed Mary of Quarr and the monks serving the Lord there, the whole company of all my men which I have in Lye and Cherc be bound for ever to grind their corn at the mill of the said monks which is situated in the land which they have from the gift of my ancestors in my fief of Cherc, nor will it be per mitted to them to grind corn anywhere else except on account of the failure of the said mill.

I have granted and conceded to the said monks and to all who often make use of the said mill free access and regress through my land.

I, Gilbert, and my heirs if ever we shall grind corn at the aforesaid mill will give the just fee just as the others'.

3. Charter of John de Visor to the Abbey of St. Mary in the Stone Quarry.

'John de Visor to all his friends and faithful ones as well present as future—greetings. Know that I have granted and in this my charter have conferred to the Lord and Abbey of St. Mary of Quarr as an everlasting alms for the salvation of my soul and of all my ancestors a certain land in my manor of Cherc. I have also granted to them to have their ship in my land free of toll and quietly and without the customary fees'.

4. An agreement between the Abbot and Convent of Ticheford (Titchfield) and the Abbot and Convent of Quarr 1266.

'Know all by whom these present writings shall be seen that whereas in the year 1266 between us the Religious, the Abbot and Convent of Ticheford of the one part and the Abbot and Convent of Quarre of the Cistercian order of the other, 2/- in the name of tithe of the Windmill which the said monks had at Cherc and arrears of the said 2/- for the tenement elapsed in which it had been in the possession of the Abbot and Convent of Ticheford, in the name of the Church . . . and certain small tithes in possession which the said monks have at Cherc, the Dean and Treasurer of Sarum being delegated by the Lord Legate, in these matters, the question arose, and after several years intervening, the question was amicably settled in this way—to wit, the said monks in good faith acknowledge having paid 2/- to the said Abbot and Convent of Ticheford and this by reason aforesaid due by them and

7

others to the said monks should peaceably be returned and the said monks should pay to the said Abbot and Convent of Ticheford the said 2/- for the same mill yearly at two terms of the year—to wit—12 pence at Michaelmas and 12 pence as long as the mill remaineth'.

These documents show the place names of Cherc (Chark) and Lye (Leya) (Lee) to be in existence. They show too a good deal of traffic across the Solent from Quarr to Titchfield Haven where the River Meon flows out. The monks of Quarr had the right to sail their boat along the coast from Titchfield Haven probably to Stokes Bay. The importance of the rights to the dues paid for the use of the mill is illustrated by the complicated legal agreement between the monks of Quarr and those of Titchfield to ensure that payment was made.

From the point of view of the historian the best day in the history of Rowner was 6th February 1277 when the Brune family became associated with the parish. On this day Edward I who spent a good deal of time in Rowner and the area around, granted to his chamberlain, William le Brun and Isolde his wife (as a marriage portion) the manor of Rowner. William le Brun was a constant attendant on the King and was with him at the Battle of Falkirk in 1298. His name, and that of his son, appear in the roll of those attached to the King's household. Isolda was a maid of honour to Queen Eleanor. The manor had become forfeited to the King by reason of a felony committed by William de la Faleyse for which he was outlawed. The descendants of the Brune family have been associated with Rowner from that time until today.

Another charter dated 18th June 1283 states that Edward I granted to William le Brun free warren in his demesne lands at Rowner and a number of other places, and another of 12th January 1288 states that the lands lately given by the King to William le Brun should be free from all charges on them by the Jews.

William le Brun died in 1300 and his wife Isolda died in 1307. In May 1292 William le Brun presented the Rectory to his son who was instituted on 11th May by Bishop John de Pontissara, but when the boy died in 1302 he was still under age and a ward of John de Wadham, Rector of Notsellinge (Nursling). In 1306 Nicholas le Brun became rector.

Grants of this kind were rarely completely free of encumbrances. In this case the new holder had to provide one man fully armed for the defence of Portchester Castle. Actually the le Bruns did not send the man but paid £2 a year to provide a substitute.

Sir William Brun, grandson of the first holder, died in 1362 and was buried at Rowner. But his body did not rest in peace. It was exhumed by his son and heir, Ingelran, and removed from the burial ground. A good deal of controversy took place about this time, and another member of the family brought an action againt Ingelran before William of Wykeham, the Bishop of Winchester.

An inquiry held on 1st September 1375 tried to obtain proof of the age of Ingelran. It was proved that he was born at Titchfield and baptised at the Chapel at Chark on 6th December in the 27th year of the reign of Edward III (1354). One set of witnesses, possibly prompted by Ingelran, proved it in this way. 'On the same 6th December one of their number acquired a certain messuage of land in the parish of Titchfield, some of the others were witnesses to the deed of acquisition and they recollected that on the same day Ingelran Bruyn was baptised'. Another set (possibly also prompted by Ingelran) avowed that a certain quarrel between the Vicar of Titchfield and Peter Bele concerning the titles of a certain garden, was made up on 6th December and on the same day, so they declared, the said Vicar baptised the said Ingelran and also they saw how his godfather, Ingelran de Dunstede, lifted him out of the holy font on the same day'. The proof of age was given before Oliver de Harnham.

For the next 150 years little more is heard of Rowner, but when in 1552 the thread of the story can be picked up again, another member of the family, Sir John Brune, is busy trying to establish his claim to Rowner.

ALVERSTOKE

Like Rowner, the story of Alverstoke goes back beyond Norman times and a record of the village is given in Domesday Book 1086. According to the Register of John de Pontissara 1280, Alverstoke derived its name from a Saxon lady, Alwara, who was supposed on the death of her husband Leowin, and in her own right, to have bestowed the manor, together with those of Exton and Widhay, on the Church of St. Swithun at Winchester for the performance of masses for the repose of his soul. The original name given in the Charter of 948 was Stoke but by 1086 it had become Alwarestock. Stock (or Stoake) means a hamlet or manor. Alwara may have been an individual of that name or a woman of the Alwara (The Al people). So Alverstoke may be a manor of the lady Alwara, or possibly the manor of the Al people.

In any case at the time of the Domesday record Alverstoke was included in the Hundred of Meonstoke and was held by the Bishops of Winchester. It was stated to have been 'conventual land' always. An old document on manorial customs states 'We (the Church) claim jurisdiction over the manor and borough and lands of Alverstoke over the sea shore, between high and low water mark and over the sea as far as a man can ride into it on a white horse at the low water time and over reach it with a lance'.

Although the manor was held by the Convent of St. Swithun in late

Saxon times, William the Conqueror seized it with other manors as a punishment on the Prior and twelve of his monks who had fought for King Harold at the fatal battle of Hastings in 1066 and bestowed it on the Bishop of Winchester. Some years later, between 1100 and 1129, William Gifford, who was Bishop of Winchester, restored Alverstoke to the monks of St. Swithun. But there was a constant feud between the Bishops of Winchester and the Priors of the Convent of St. Swithun. In 1282 there is, for example, a record of John de Pontissara, who was Bishop of Winchester, resigning the advowson of Alverstoke to the monks, although reserving for himself certain rights of patronage. In this document the manor is described as Alwarestock-cum-Goseport. Right down to 1537 we find records of first the Bishops and then the Priors being in control of the manor.

What was the manor, about which there was so much controversy, really like? In the famous Domesday Survey, made in 1086, as a basis for the collection of taxes, Alverstoke was included in the Hundred of Meonstoke. The record describes Alverstoke thus. 'In the time of Edward the Confessor, it was assess d at 16 hides, but King Edward reduced it to 10 hides and so it remained. It was, and is now held, by villeins in number 48, who occupy fifteen ploughlands. It was and is still worth £6. One Knight holds half a hide of this manor, which was assessed with other hides. Sawinus held it, but was not allowed to dwell elsewhere. Here is one ploughfield with two borderers worth 25/-'. There is no reference to a church but it is almost certain that there was in fact a church in Saxon times. Bearings taken in the 19th century show that the original church at Alverstoke was not built due E—W but NE—SW as was the case with a number of Saxon churches. The reduction in the assessment from 16 hides in Edward's reign to 10 hides in 1086 suggests that the value of the manor was declining. But is it possible that Alverstoke may have suffered from Viking raids? The fall in the value of the manor of Fareham was deliberately attributed to the pillage of the Vikings.

The next we hear of Alverstoke is in 1282 when Andrew, Prior of St. Swithun's Convent, granted a Magna Charter or Charter of Liberty of the Parish of Alverstoke, giving the inhabitants of the liberty and freedom of Alward Stoake, release from certain taxes and dues and from their state of serfdom. All this was in return for money payments. There is also a report that Alwarestock is one of the manors for the return of whose writs and other liberties, a charter was granted by John, Bishop of Winchester in 1283.

The Charter granted by Andrew de Londonia, Prior of the Convent of St. Swithun is a most interesting document. It freed the men of Alverstoke (including Gosport), Bury, Brockhurst and Forton from the state of serfdom. With the charter was granted a seal. It was a circular seal, two and a half inches in diameter. In the centre was represented an episcopal figure seated, having a low mitre on his head, holding in his right hand a pastoral staff and in his left a book, the cover of which had four round studded bosses and represents the Gospels. Round the edge of the seal was an inscription SIGILL: COMVNE: HOMINVM: PRIORIS: SCI SWITHVNI: DE: ALWARESTOKE. The figure is almost certainly that of Andrew de Londinia and the translation is probably 'This is the Seal of St. Swithun's belonging to the Tenants of Alverstoke'. This translation was made in 1606 and there is a note saying that on the 22nd November 1606 in the reign of King James 1st 'the originall of the deede or charter within written remained the daie and yeare above written in the handes and custodie of Robert Mathew of Brockhurst with the seale fayer to the said deed belonging. Together alsoe with the sylver seale within mentioned and likewise an exemplification under the broad seale granted in Kinge Edwardes tyme the fowerth which deed and exemplification was had to London the daie and yeare aforesaid by the said Robert Mathew, Thomas Bonner, Francis Thorney and Thomas Watts'. But of the seal itself no trace remains.

It is worth setting out the charter almost in full.

'To all Christian people to whom a knowledge of this present Charter shall come: Andrew, by Divine permission, Prior of the Convent of St. Swithun, at Winchester, sends health in the Lord.

'Know ye, that we of our own free will and consent, have granted, and by this present charter have confirmed to all our men or tenants of our manor of Alwardstoake, that they and their posterity shall be free for ever, as well as from fining or being taxed, as also from paying any rental or salt due; and from Chircheset or Kirke—sida-fle, and of having their swine taken for pannage or sums of money, for the King's service in war or urgent occasions, sometimes called Tallagis.

'And it shall henceforward be lawful for them to make their wills, and freely dispose of their goods, and their children. And they shall be free from warrants and suits to the Courts of the Hundreds, save only within Alwardstoake.

'Also, we grant unto them, all the lands which they now hold, to have and to hold to them and their heirs, and to whosoever they give or assign the same, freely and without disturbance by lawful inheritance for ever, so as by such their gift, sale or assignment, there be no impeachment, nor hindrance unto us or to our church in our rights.

'In consideration of which, this our Grant and Charter, the said tenants with one assent and consent have agreed to pay unto us, and to our successors, and to our Church of St. Swithun at Winchester four pence for each acre with the appurtenance for all the lands of the manor, four times in the year, at the feast of All-Saints one penny; and at the feast of the purification of our Blessed Lady, one penny; and at the feast of the Holy Cross, one penny; and at the feast of St. Michael, one penny for every acre of land of the said manor, to be measured by the pole of sixteen feet and a half.

'Except always that for all the land which is betwixt the two waters, from the water course where the mill of the almoner of our church is situated, unto that other water course which runneth under the orchard of the parsons of Alverstoke, for which the tenants of Stoake, Forton, Brockhurst and Bury, shall pay for every acre six pennies yearly, at every one of the terms before mentioned, one penny and a half, except a yardlande and a half which is betwixt the bounds of the same water courses for which they shall pay, for every acre, yearly four pennies, at every one of the terms days aforesaid, for every acre one penny. And every one of the tenants of the said manor after the death of his ancestor, shall give to pay for his holding of the land, so much as he pays yearly for rent.

'Moreover we have granted to our said tenants, that at the first coming of us, or of our steward, to hold a court after the feast day of St. Michael they chuse three of the most efficient and discreet men among them, of the said manor, whom they shall present to us or to our steward, to the end we may make choice of one of them, to be our Boroughreeve or Bailiff for the year, and that year being ended, they shall then chuse and present out of which in likewise we or our steward may appoint one to be our bailiff, who shall take the oath on the Holy Evangelists, that he shall faithfully levy and seize all manorial suits, excheats and forfeitures as well great and small and present the same to us at our next coming, or to our steward, without concealment of any. To the end according to the law of the land, they may be taken, in such sort notwithstanding as the duties and profits thereof arising, be always preserved and reserved to us and our church.

'And it is further agreed betwist us and our said tenants that all manners of controversies and pleadings shall be pleaded and tried without delay in the court of Alwardstoake either before us, or in the presence of our steward, without any suing out of the King's writs; so as the same be done according to the laws and customs of this realm of England according to such course as freeholders of the shire do observe, so shall everyone recover his right in our court and not otherwise unless he finds that there justice be not rightly minstered unto him: nevertheless they shall appear when summoned before the King's Justices of the Assize thereto to answer as they were wont to do.

'In witness whereof to this present charter indented like a fine to that part which remaineth with the tenants of Alwardstoake we have affixed the seal of our conventual church and to the other parts indented which remaineth in our Convent. Signed Thomas de Forton,

Richard Bishopp, Henry son of Pranett, Robert Bishopp, Robert son of Arnold and John Pennie, for and in the names of all the rest of the tenant of the whole manor, with one assent and consent have set all their seals'.

The first boroughreeve to be appointed under the terms of the charter was Thomas de Forton.

The vital point about the charter is its evidence of a decline in serfdom and its restrictions. The tenants were to be free. This is a very good example of the change from payment in kind to payment in money, from tribute in crops and livestock to payment of rent. The tenants were to be free from tribute of corn, from produce from the soil, from payment of three hens, a capon or cock and at Easter a hundred eggs or from having their swine taken. There were personal freedoms, too—they could apprentice their sons, they could make them priests, their daughters could marry without the consent of the lord and the payment of a fine. A widow could marry again without obtaining consent from the lord. There was right to sell a stallion or a bull. There was the right to dispose of one's tenement or land. All these irksome restrictions which had been the normal lot of the peasantry were now removed although the lord claimed and retained many social privileges. It is interesting to notice too that some of the land, the richer and more fertile soil between the waters—the river Alver in the south and the Forton creek—was charged at a higher rate for each acre. The right to appoint a Boroughreeve brought the first rudiments of local self-government although until the early 19th century the local court at Alverstoke was that presided over by the Steward on behalf of the Lord of the Manor—in later years the Bishop of Winchester.

But although there was personal freedom within the manor, the Prior of St. Swithun's still had jurisdiction and could enforce any duties the villagers might have collectively. When for example Fareham was granted a borough court and a boroughreeve in 1337 it was noted 'The town of Alverstoke which belongs to the Prior of St. Swithun must send 95 men on the summons of the bailiff of Fareham for one boon day in autumn to reap the Bishop's corn. If so be they come late to work or work badly they must be fined by the bailiff and if rain or any other hindrance prevent them from doing the day's work they must come on the morrow and from day to day until they have finished a full day's work'. It must have been a sight worth witnessing—the reluctant tenants from Alverstoke trudging to Fareham to do boon work on the Bishop's land at harvest time.

An inquiry was made into the parish and manor of Alverstoke in 1341. 'On Wednesday the first week in Lent 1341 an inquisition was taken at Winchester before the Abbot of Beaulieu and his followers. Returned by oath of Robert Upton, William Stormy, Ralph

13

Worplesdene, Henryatte Dane, William Jordan, William Cnewyne, John Aubreye, William le Lont, William Smallheech and John de Taylour. That the ninths of this parish of Alverstoke came to £101 1s. 3d. There were no traders in this parish, all the inhabitants lived by agriculture or hand labour and the ecclesiastical person had temporalities in this parish. The Rectory was endowed with land worth six marks and a yearly rental of 10/-, pasture worth 26/8, privileges of exempt jurisdiction 30/-, tithes of dovecots 6/8, small tithes of pease, hemp, flax, turves, calves, pigs, broom, etc., £6 19s. 7d. Formerly there were 15 ships great and small which paid tithes to the rector'.

GOSPORT

The story associated with the name God's Port goes back about 150 years before 1283, the date of the charter of the men of Alverstoke, into the reign of King Stephen (1135-1154). Stephen was the monarch who seized the throne on the death of Henry I, his uncle. His only claims were first that he was the son of William the Conqueror's daughter, and second that Henry I had intended that his daughter Matilda should succeed him. There ensued a long period of bitter civil war. Stephen's reign has been described as '19 long winters'. Walter Map writing shortly after says of Stephen 'Of outstanding skill in arms but in other things almost an idiot except he was more inclined to evil'. The story is told that on returning from Normandy, Stephen was caught in a fierce storm off Spithead and was rescued by local fishermen who brought him into the quiet water of the harbour. In return for their bravery and loyalty, the King's half-brother, Henry de Blois, then Bishop of Winchester, granted a charter to the inhabitants allowing them to hold two fairs each year, one on 4th May and the other on the 10th October, and the right to have three market days a week. According to this tradition the place was henceforth to be known as God's Port. There are of course several versions of the story. The one I have cited would date the naming of the town about 1144. Other versions suggest that it was the Bishop of Winchester himself who landed on the beaches after a furious storm and built the church at Alverstoke giving to the whole area the name of God's Port. That explains, so some say, why there is no mention of a church at Alverstoke in the Domesday Book of 1086.

Stephen's predecessor, Henry I, was in Rowner in September 1114 and the record shows that he departed from Portsmouth by ship shortly afterwards. Nearly 20 years later, in 1133, when Henry I made his last expedition to France, a curious incident occurred. A writer who was present says 'Whilst the King was waiting there suddenly appeared clouds in the sky of such magnitude as had never been seen before in England. The King and his attendants, astonished at the sudden darkness, looking towards the sun saw it appear like a new moon. Several stars appeared and while the ships were ready to receive the King, the sea being calm, and only a gentle breeze of wind, the large anchors of one of the ships were suddenly moved by some unseen cause out of the ground, so that she drove against the next, to the astonishment of all that beheld it, and, notwithstanding all their efforts to prevent it, eight ships were dashed together so that nothing of them remained'. The King, in gratitude for deliverance, founded a church at Portchester.

In 1282 John de Pontissara (Bishop of Winchester 1280-1304) records resigning the advowsons of Drokensford, Havonte and Alwarstock-cum-Goseport to the jurisdiction of the Abbot and Convent of St. Swithun's. This is the first official reference to the name of Gosport.

We do know too that in 1682 a fire-heath receipt describes the place as Godsport. This receipt was discovered in the beam of an old house in the High Street, Gosport, when it was pulled down in August 1833. The receipt is written thus: 'Received of Edward King, the sum of four shillings in full for one half year's duty for four fire-hearths in this house in Godsport due and ended at Michlemas last past. I say received by Edward Nevey, Collector'. But it may be that the collector was better at gathering in taxes than at spelling. There is little doubt about the authenticity of the receipt—the hearth tax which was imposed in 1662 was much objected to and was abolished in 1689.

Not much was done by the local community to retain the idea of God's Port until shortly after the last war (1939-45). Indeed in an Act of Parliament of 1811 granting permission for the building of the market hall, it is declared that the rights of holding the annual fairs had been purchased by the inhabitants from the Bishop of Winchester—but which Bishop and which inhabitants is not stated. But the name God's Port is now firmly established. When the Borough Council was anxious to obtain a new coat of arms, we were asked to produce a number of specimen mottoes and to endeavour to retain the conception of God's Port. The one actually selected was one of about six submitted, 'God's Port our Haven'.

Of course there are other explanations for the name. One is that it was originally Gossport derived from the furze, gorse or goss which covered the shores in a blaze of yellow bloom. People who accept this view quote from Shakespeare's 'Tempest' 'Tooth'd briers, sharp furzes, pricking goss and thorns'. And others suggest Goseport—from the geese that lived on the low lying waters of the inland creeks. This explanation, which suggests that Gosport was the market place where geese were sold, seems to go back to the 13th century and is perhaps as near the truth as anyone will ever get.

Throughout the rest of the Middle Ages little is known of Gosport. There are no charters, no records of famous people. In 1341 there is a reference that only those 'who live by agriculture or by land labour' live there.

BEDENHAM

North of Alverstoke, and on either side of the main road running to Fareham, with a muddy coastline facing the upper reaches of Portsmouth harbour lies Bedenham, which, since it was acquired by the Admiralty in 1913, has been part of the Royal Naval Armament Depot. Its history is closely linked with Alverstoke and with Rowner.

Originally Bedenham (or Bedeham) was a small Saxon (or Jutish) manor attached to the larger manor of Alverstoke. It is mentioned in Domesday Book in 1086 as being assessed at half a hide and being worth 25/-. There was one team (plough team) and two bordmen (cottage land labourers). In 1086 it was held by a certain 'Miles'.

We hear again about Bedenham in the early 14th century when there must have been a fair sized farm house in the manor. In 1303 John de Drokensford who held Bedenham, and who some five years later was to be instituted as Bishop of Bath and Wells, bestowed the manor and the advowson of Bedenham church on one, Roger Lancelene for life. The church was referred to as the 'oratory' of the house at Bedenham in Alverstoke and was probably a chapel licensed for worship within the manor house. When Roger Lancelene died the property reverted to John de Drokensford who held it until he died in May 1329. John's brother, who was named Philip and was the heir to the estate, held it until his death in 1356 when it was left to Margaret his wife.

Margaret married again, this time to Maurice le Brun of Rowner and this brought the fortunes of Bedenham into association with Rowner which since 1277 had been held by the Brun family. But the ownership of Bedenham was a frequent source of dispute for centuries to come.

There seeams to have been a good deal of controversy within the Brun family arising from the complicated land settlements of the period. On 13th June 1358 an inquiry was held concerning a settlement made by Sir William Bruyne (a grandson of the original William le Brun to whom the manor had been granted by Edward I in 1277). In this inquiry it was held that the first William le Brun had granted the manor and advowson of Rowner to John de Overton, in trust for the said William le Brun for life and then for William, the son of Thomas Wayte and his wife Johanna (daughter of the said William le Brun) and if dying without heirs the property should return to the rightful heirs of William le Brun.

The value of the manor of Rowner was £8 3s. 0d. a year and the value of the benefice 10 marks. The inquiry also mentions that the same

William le Brun held, withing the Hundred of Titchfield a certain 'Liberty' called Crofton of the value of 18/– and held it from the Earl of Richmond.

CHAPTER 2

Gosport, Alverstoke and Rowner in Tudor times. 1485-1603

In this chapter something is told of the life of Gosport during the Tudor period from 1485, when Henry VII came to the throne, until the death of Elizabeth I in 1603. It was nationally a period of momentous change. The colleges at Oxford were seething with new learning, printing was becoming fashionable, the church was reformed by Henry VIII's decrees, a new world of exploration opened up and the long grim struggle with the might of Spain came to its climax with the Armada. Locally these stirring events made little impact.

On August 9th 1552, the 14 year-old Edward VI crossed Portsmouth Harbour in a small boat to view the defences. He noted in his diary: 'In the morning I went to Chaterton bulwarke and viewed also the toune. At afternoune went to see the Storehouse and ther toke a bote and went to the wodden toure and so to Haselford. Upon viewing of wich things ther was devised tow fortes to be made upon the entry of the haven, one where Ridlei's Toure standith, upon the neke that makith the camber the other upon a like neke standing on the tother side the haven where stode an old bulwarke of wode. This was devised for the strength of the haven. It was ment that that to touneside should be stronger and larger'.

Later he wrote to his friend Barnaby Fitzpatrick: 'The haven noteable great and standing by Nature easy to be fortified, and for the more strength thereof we have devised two castellis on either side of the Haven at the mouth thereof". The young king died within the year and the changed political situation meant that his rebuilding plans were never carried out.

The important document of this period however, is that of Leland. Every now and then in English history there appears a great traveller journalist who loves touring and describing the countryside. Daniel Defoe was one of these, William Cobbett another. Even in our own generation we enjoy sound and television programmes of travels around the countryside. Leland was one of these journalist wanderers—nothing missed him and in his famous work 'Itineries' he describes his journeys. He was writing early in the reign of Henry VIII, i.e., at the beginning of the 16th century. This is what he says: 'From Titchfield to Gosport, a little village of Fisschar Men by much hethy and feren ground of VI (6) miles. Here stood a prophanid (ruined) Chapelle near the shore of Portsemouth Haven scant half a mile from the very mouth of the Haven. The lande on the west Pointe of Portsemouth Haven is a sandy nesse and some brekith of gyving place to the open Se. There is a round Tourre with ordinaunce at the West Pointe of the Mouth of Portsemouth Haven, and a little way uppe to the haven is a great creke goying by west up into the lande a mile called Ostrepole Lake. Scant a quarter of a mile above this is Gosport Village'. Ostrepole (Oyster pool) if of course Haslar Creek.

Leland continues 'About a quarter of a mile above this village is another 'creke' called Forton, a little village by it. A mile and a half above this is Bedenham Creke, so called of a village standing by it'.

Leland listened to a lot of gossip. He goes on, 'I learned in the toune (Portsmouth) that the tourres in the Haven Mouth were begun in King Edward IV tyme and set forward in building by Richard III. King Henry VIII ended them at the procuration of Fox, Bishop of Winchester. King Henry VII of late tyme sette in Portsemouth capitaines of certain soldiers in Garrison'.

This then is Gosport, a small fisher village near an oyster lake or creek and with sandy waste heath land. Go to Clayhall and Haslar and use your imagination and you can picture Gosport as Leland did 450 years ago.

Indeed Leland's account is confirmed by a picture dated 1545. In that year off St. Helen's Point in the Isle of Wight, the French Fleet anchored. There was no great battle but a permanent record was made in some paintings in fresco at Cowdray House in Sussex. One of them showed the harbour and on the Gosport side three circular forts each with two tiers of cannon. Engravings of the picture have been made— one is in Gosport Town Hall, another in a Committee Room at Winchester.

Another writer says that a round tower was built at the south west point of the bay. Ships could be moored there to shelter from the wind and that part of the Harbour was called 'Little Paradise'. It is now the main submarine base.

We have no information as to the way in which the villagers of Alverstoke, Gosport or Rowner reacted to the religious changes of the 16th century. Records were kept indifferently and we have to be satisfied with occasional glimpses. In 1511, shortly before the great religious storm, a curious inventory was made of the goods and ornaments belonging to St. Mary's Church at Alverstoke—

'One Kanyte of Silke, and two of nydell-work to hang ye pyn on: three lynnyn trimors stayned with other stynes: four coffers and two peyer of harness: two hangings of dormer for the low aulters: two hangings of blew chamlett and lawney: one gyrdell of green sylke with buckill studd and penden of sylver: one beadsmans bell, four rynges silver, one paull of cloth of Criwell: one banner clothe of sylke with a perlow of red sylke: eight Krehets: a pane of wood printed and two rochatts for the clerkes'.

Records tend to be preserved better where they relate to grants of ownership of property or where there is a continuity of family interest. But even in Rowner where the family association has remained since 1277 there is a gap of nearly 200 years in the history. But on the 24th February 1554, there is a record of the grant by Sir Oliver Wallope and Henry, his son and heir apparent to Sir John Brune concerning a yearly rent of twelve pounds out of a Grange called Charke in the parish of Rowner. We are at once brought back to the Brune family. The bond accompanying the charter states—

'The condycon of this oblygecon ys suche that where the 10th in bounden Sir Olyvere Wallope by his Dede having late of these present hath bargand, sold, demysed, relesed and quiet claymed for him and his heires with the within named Sir John Bruine all his ryght title interest demande in and to one yerely Rent of 12 pounds, comynge and goynge out of one grange and farm callyd Charke and beynge in the pyoshe of Rowner, in the countie of Sutht as by the sayd Dede of the same Sir Olyvere thereof made unto the said Sir John Bruine'.

Shortly before, on 16th November 1552, Sir John Brune had sat down to write a long letter to Sir William Cecil concerning a dispute about the tenure of some of his estates. The letter is a priceless human document illustrating the difficulty of establishing and dealing with claims when records were kept so indifferently—

'My humble commendations done, yet may please you to be advised, I cannot yet as find my pedigree whereof I am very sorry, for as much as I am not able to acccomplish your request in that behalf. Sir, I have sent you by this beerer a book wherein is contained much of the conveyances concerning my inheritance and therein is also a pedigree of my late ancestors with the entail concerning a title of lands which at this present I sue for, and the daughters of one Henry Brune mentioned in the said pedigree had the same lands, the lands being entailed to the other males of the Brunes as more plainly it may appear by the said book: if it may be your pleasure to see the same pedigree I shall be very glad thereof, in consideration of my present suit concerning that matter, it may please you that my servant may have the book delivered again, who shall attend your leisure for the same, this having to trouble you with my rude learning. I commend you to the Lord, who preserve you with increase of much honour, from my house at Rowner, the 16th day of November 1552. Yours assuredly to command, John Brune'.

Fortunately, too, we have a copy of the will of this Sir John Brune whose tomb, dated 1559, is a striking feature of Rowner Church. The will is dated 28th August 1559, which sheds a good deal of light not only upon that lovable personality but on conditions in Rowner at that period—

'I, John Brune, of Rowner, County of Southampton, Knight, being sick of body but thanks be to Almighty God, of good and perfect memory, do declare, ordain and make this my last will and testament in manner and form following. First I bequeath my soul unto Almighty God, our Blessed Lady and all the holy company of heaven and my body to be buried in the parish church of Rowner, within my own chapel there, upon which church and chapel I will shall be bestowed by my executrix for the repairing of the same the sum of £6, and also I will there shall be bestowed upon the making of my tomb the sum of £10. I will that my executrix cause me to be buried in such sort and order as to the degree of a Knight doth of ancient custom appertain'.

Then he bequeathed to Winchester Cathedral 6/8, to the church at Rowner a decent cope of black velvet to the value of £5, the same to be bought within a month of his burial, otherwise the said £5 to be expended on the repairing of Rowner Church. To the poor of Fareham, Titchfield, Portsmouth, Stoke and Rowner—to be prayed for £10. To the Queen's Highness (Queen Elizabeth I) with the wardship of his heir during his minority, his manor of Rowner with his lands in Alverstoke of the clear value of £28 8s. 6d. For the building of a manor house at Rowner and for the marriage of his heir £400, the said sum to be laid out by his wife with the advice of his other overseers and executors. 'But if the wardship and marriage cannot be obtained, and be given to some other person, that the said sum of £400 be kept and saved until he come of full age and then be delivered to him for the repairing of the said house'. He gave to his son and heir, Henry Brune, all his furniture at his house at Rowner, half his plate, 400 Sheep, 34 Kyne, a cart furnished with six horses and four edging horses, 12 oxen, 30 quarters of wheat and 30 quarters of barley and all other corn, grain and other things appertaining to his house and demesnes of Rowner, and in his grange called Charke and his lease of the parsonage of Stoke.

But if the story of Leland's tour gives an interesting picture of Gosport in the early 1500 period, the next document is far more exciting. It is a decree made in the 44th year of the reign of Queen Elizabeth (1602) concerning the right to the Ferry between Gosport and Portsmouth. Here we have the best record of all. It gives the names of local residents, relates the difficulties of crossing the harbour, prescribes how many boats were to be available and how they were to be handled. It even gives the fares to be charged.

This document is a decree made by the Court of Exchequer at Southampton. The plaintiffs in this strange case were Roger Trynlett, John Chesle and Erasmus Burges described as inhabitants of Gosport and tenants unto the Right Reverend Father in God Thomas now Bishop of Winchester, as well for themselves as for and in the behalf of all other tenants and inhabitants of the said town of Gosport'. The defendants were Stephen Riddleson and John Jeffrys. The cause of the action 'being or and concerning a ferry or sea passage between the town of Gosport and the town of Portsmouth, claimed by the plaintiffs and other tenants of Gosport as appurtenant and belonging unto their several freelands or tenaments in Gosport aforesaid, and contrarywise the defendants make title thereunto by lease from Her Majesty' for which leave or exclusive monopoly of the rights of the ferry the defendant, Stephen Riddleson, paid a rent.

Here was indeed an issue. Who owned the ferry? Did it belong by immemorial custom to the inhabitants of Gosport at large, or to a single group with a royal charter? Who says history is dull and uninteresting when in 1602 the contestants joined issue on this important matter.

After hearing all the evidence of witnesses and studying all the claims of the parties concerned, the Court came to the conclusion that the plaintiffs and the other tenants of Gosport 'have for the space of divers years past used the said ferry or sea passage to carry and recarry the inhabitants of the said town of Gosport as well as others of Her Majesty's subjects and passengers as also all such provisions as are usually transported from Gosport aforesaid to the said town of Portsmouth for Her Majesty's service, and the particular good of the said County of Southampton'. The Court therefore was of the opinion 'that it was not expedient for the commonwealth, nor for the safety of the said town of Portsmouth that the ferry or sea passage should be under the rule and direction of any one man, but that the same should be at liberty to be used as before time had been'.

It was therefore ordered by the Court on the 28th January 1601 'that the said John Riddleson, Her Majesty's farmer (i.e., the one to whom it had been farmed out) of the said ferry or sea passage should forthwith bring into Court the lease by him obtained of the said ferry or sea passage, to be cancelled'. It was further ordered that a Commission should be set up to call before them the principal inhabitants of Gosport, Alverstoke, Portsmouth in order to control the ferry. The names of the Commissioners were Sir Handen Paulett, Sir William Avedale, Francis Cotten and John White.

When they met they discovered, to use their own words 'that time, whereof the memory of man is not to the contrary, the said ferry and sea passage hath been maintained and kept by the inhabitants of the said borough of Gosport only and they they have usually taken of every footman passing in their boats over unto Portsmouth one halfpenny and so much for passing back again; and if any footman pass over alone he paid one penny, and that by the said use and continuance of the said ferry and sea passage at Gosport, there hath been from time to time, and was at the time making the said certificate, good store of sufficient sea-faring men and mariners bred up and maintained there in marine affairs to the great furtherance of Her Majesty's service at the seas'.

Picture the indignation of the men of Gosport when John Riddleson declared that he had the exclusive right (for which he had paid a rent) to the control of the ferry.

The four Commissioners came to the conclusion 'that the inhabitants of the said borough of Gosport should still continue the use of the said ferry and sea passage, taking for fare according to the usual rate aforesaid, and no more. And (they went on) to the end the said ferry and sea passage may at all times be furnished with a convenient number of serviceable boats, to serve for such ordinary travellers as shall daily pass there, to be in readiness for transporting, aid of men and other necessities for the relief of the town of Portsmouth and the Isle of Wight upon every sudden attempt, they, the said Commissioners, thought it meet that there should always be maintained by the inhabitants there the number of twenty good and serviceable boats as well for horse as men, and of them there should be daily attending for transporting ordinary travellers five, whereof three to be such as should be meet for the passing of horsemen, and that one of the said boats should daily attend upon the shore of Portsmouth side; and for avoiding the many dangers that through negligence or disorder of the passengermen might grow to the hazard and prejudice of the passengers there, the said Commissioners thought it meet, that there should be made choice of two of the substantialest inhabitants of the said borough to be nominated once every year at their law day held there; and that they together with the constable for the time being, should take charge that all the said boats be kept in good strong and serviceable sort well able to brooke the seas; and that no passenger boats be suffered to pass over with any passenger without one skilful and able man at the least to take charge thereof, and that there be no disorder, or exacting more of the passengers than ordinary prices'.

And so it was therefore ordered and decreed by the Court of Exchequer in 1602 'that the inhabitants of the said borough of Gosport and their heirs, free tenants unto the said Bishop of Winchester shall from henceforward still hold and continue the use of the said ferry or sea passage as appurtenant and belonging unto their several freelands or tenements in Gosport aforesaid, without let or disturbance of any person or persons whatsoever and from time to time keep and maintain twenty good, able and serviceable boats, sufficiently and well furnished, to carry and recarry all passengers, as well horsemen as footmen, and all other provisions passing between the said borough of Gosport and town of Portsmouth; and every of the same boats to have one skilful and able man, at the least, to take charge of every such boat for the more safe and surer transporting of every passenger, their horses, and other provisions, taking for every footman passing in their boats over to Portsmouth one halfpenny and for passing back again one halfpenny, and for every footman passing alone a penny, and no more or greater sum to be paid by any person or persons'.

It was also ordered and decreed by the court that there 'should be always continually and from time to time attending five good and serviceable boats at the least of the twenty said boats, well provided, whereof three shall be for the transporting of footmen, and one of these five at the least, shall be continually on that side of the water next unto the town of Portsmouth, to the end that passengers shall not be delayed or hindered on their journey'.

Finally the court ordered and decreed that 'for avoiding the many dangers that may grow by the negligence, disorder and unskilfulness of the men that shall have the guiding, rule and oversight of the said passenger boats . . . it is thought fit that the inhabitants of the said Borough of Gosport for the time being shall from henceforth have power and authority yearly at their law days holden for the said borough to elect and chuse two honest, substantial and skilful men amongst themselves, who, together with the constables of the said borough for the time being, shall take upon them the care and charge, that the number of boats above mentioned shall always be in readiness furnished as aforesaid, with able and sufficient persons for the well guiding of the same boats and carrying and recarrying of passengers, horses, and other provisions acccording to the true meaning of this decree; and shall likewise have power and authority, by virtue thereof, to punish according to their discretion all and every such person and persons as shall offend, either by disorderly behaviour of themselves towards the passengers or their carriages or by taking any greater rate or rates of the pasengers than is above mentioned'.

This document is a fascinating study of the practical local problems raised by the conflict about monopolies at the beginning of the 17th century. It shows a demand for local justice on the basis of immemorial custom and rights. It speaks of Gosport as a separate town, indeed as a borough, for the first time. It shows that the crossing of the harbour was becoming a matter of importance commercially. The sturdy townsmen of the time were prepared to defend their rights even against the Crown and the courts were prepared to support their claim. Obviously by 1600 we are far advanced from Leland's description of a small fishing village of less than a century before.

CHAPTER 3

When Gosport and Portsmouth were at War

The growing importance of the western side of Portsmouth Harbour is shown in two incidents which occurred during the early Stuart period. In November 1606 the local inhabitants of Alverstoke, headed by Robert Mathews, Thomas Bruner, Francis Thorney and Thomas Watts managed to secure a translation of the original charter of freedom of the men of Alverstoke dated 1282. They visited London and "there found the said deed and exemplification verbatim word for word faier written in the Toure of London in the Rowles. And the said Thomas Bruner, Francis Thorney and Thomas Watts have taken the true copies thereof under their handes ether to other". At a time when the men of Gosport had asserted their rights to the harbour ferry, they were obviously anxious to secure their claims to manage their own affairs. This is an interesting example of a popular movement to base the rights of the local community upon the immemorial grants and charters of earlier centuries. It shows that the problems which were agitating the minds of the politicians and lawyers in London were being discussed also by the gentry in local districts.

By 1620 serious thought was being given to the condition of the navy. One of the purposes of the extension of the Ship Money tax to inland towns was to improve the standard of naval ship contruction and harbour facilities. In 1627 a survey was carried out on the western side of Portsmouth harbour, particularly in the area around Forton, to ascertain its suitability for dockyard purposes. The scheme was not proceeded with at the time and only after another 125 years was the same area acquired for the construction of a naval store-yard. Meanwhile on the 14th July, 1628, a grant was made by Charles I to Robert Pamplin of all the mud lands lying between high-water and low-water marks along the coast of Hampshire from Hayling Island to Lymington and beyond. The grant excluded the liberties of the corporate body of Portsmouth but included among other areas "a certain place called Hoeford, a bridge called Wallington Bridge, the town of Gosport, the castle called Halesworth Castle (later Haslar), and a certain place called Browndean Beacons". The real purpose of the grant was to promote schemes for the reclamation of large areas of low lying land. Once reclaimed the better land would be subject to a rental payment of 4 pence per acre, and the poorer land to ½d. an acre payable to the Crown. Robert Pamplin had two daughters, one of them, Mary, married Sir George Wandesford, the other—Margaret—married William Wandesford, so that in time the whole grant came under the control of the Wandesford family and was known as the Wandesford grant. It shows that consideration was being given at the time not only to the extension of the dockyard to the western side of the harbour but to extensive reclamation of whole areas of mud flats within Portsmouth harbour, although in fact little reclamation took place at the time. Years later towards the end of the 18th century the Wandesford grant became the basis of a prolonged legal case in the High Courts concerning the right of contractors to erect wharves and warehouses within the harbour.

The great Civil War between the Royalists (led by Charles I) and the Parliamentarians (or Roundheads) broke out in 1642. It was the culmination of a period of strife as bitter as any in the history of our country. It is not proposed to tell the story of those perilous years, nor to discuss the causes of the quarrel. But there is a good record of the conflict as it affected Gosport. Generally, at the time of the outbreak, the citadal of Portsmouth was being held for the King, and Gosport and the area around was almost to a man for Parliament. The siege and surrender of Portsmouth was one of the most important incidents in the early part of the war and largely determined its outcome.

The King raised his standard at Nottingham on August 22nd, 1642, but even before that, on 2nd August, 1642, Lord Goring declared war on the King's behalf at Portsmouth which he then held. Goring was a capable soldier but an unprincipled scoundrel who had made promises to and received support from both sides. He had betrayed the Queen, obtained considerable sums from Parliament on the pretence that he was preparing the defence of Portsmouth against the King, even got himself appointed Lieutenant General of the Horse in the Parliament army and then finally declared that he was holding Portsmouth on behalf of the King. It was not a very wise decision for Portsmouth was badly garrisoned and poorly equipped. There were only about 300 soldiers and as many townsmen available and only about two days food supply. Goring had plenty of money since he had obtained £5,000 from Parliament and £9,000 from the Queen. For the first few days there were wild rumours of French and other foreign aid, desertions and spies, and attempts to get in food supplies.

To the people of Gosport it must have been a stirring time. The Earl of Warwick arrived with five ships on the 8th August to blockade the harbour, and a force was hastily assembled to attack the City from the north. On the 10th August, Pochdown (Portsdown) was stormed.

Goring withdrew into the city, pillaging Portsea Island with its 2,000 acres of standing corn, its 1,000 sheep and 1,000 cattle.

Attempts were made to bring in further supplies to the beleaguered garrison. On the 12th August, 1642, a load of 135 quarters of wheat was being taken from Fareham to Portsmouth, but the wagons were stopped by a few watchmen led by Master Allen of Gosport. The wheat never reached Portsmouth. Lord Goring was mad with rage. He hurled insults across the harbour and determined to bombard Gosport and utterly destroy it. The people were terrified. It was said that only after humble prayers upon his knees was the Mayor able to spare the worst. Goring called for a "Cannoner" and ordered him to fire. After a lot of argument a shot was sent across the harbour and over the houses and did no harm. It was a dangerous district in those days. The populace hated Goring but it was difficult to escape. Three gallant gentlemen, a story is told, set out in a hired boat for Stokes Bay but eventually found themselves in Chichester.

Six days later on the 18th August 1642 there were seven ships in the harbour, including the "Paragon", the "Caesar", the "Black James"— all bombarding the city. Someone on board the "Paragon" wrote that the greatest harmony was the thundering of cannon both day and night.

On that same day, the 18th August, dwellers in Portsmouth could hear the noise of pickaxes and carts in Gosport and could plainly see in that "little Village half a mile over the water from the town, the Parliamentary Forces framing some workes to make a Fort". "Whereat (continues the record) the Governour was much troubled and presently shot at them from all his workes that lay that way-ward, letting fly that night at least 60 bullets, but hurt but one man therewith, and that by his owne folly, for he stood on his workes with a candle and lanthorn in his hand, whereby they had a right aime and so shot him". Another version says that this man was Peter Baker, "a very good ship carpenter" and that he was shot by a sentry in mistake. Another record says it was John Baker and there was an entry in the register of St. Mary's Alverstoke, confirming this. "John Baker of Gosport killed by a shot from Portsmouth, August 24th, 1642".

"But for all this", writes the Chronicler of the Parliamentarians, "ours desisted not, but went on day and night until they had perfected two plat formes the one behind a Barne for 10 pieces of Ordnance, the other behind a pile of Faggots for 2 pieces, though the Governour shot incessantly 14 days and 14 nights to have beaten them off, but could not. Shortly after this a parley was sounded but without any good successe; so then they fell to it again, the Governour letting flie his ordnance apace day and night, but not with any losse to us (blessed be the Lord for it), no not a man or horse. All this time, there being but 2 pieces of Ordnance planted on the small worke of Gosport, behind the Faggots (which is still standing on the beach), which played not at all on the Towne, though they could have done it, but some short time after they shot thence and killed one of the Garison Souldiers on their Mount, and cut off a French man's leg near unto him above the Knee, to the endangering of his life. The Governour himselfe and the Lord Wentworth in their own persons (and all who could be spared from other duties) wrought all one night to make a trench on the top of the Mount, that at the sight of the firing of our Ordnance they mighty leap down into it and save themselves from the like shot at Gosport".

The last fortnight in August, 1642, was an exciting period and on the 28th and 29th, more shots were fired damaging the tower of the Cathedral and destroying one of its bells. Even after the fall of Portsmouth to the Parliamentarians, Gosport suffered during the war, especially on the dreadful night of the 6th January, 1645, when at 6 p.m. the town was plundered and many houses burned.

It was on the 28th August, 1642, that the guns from the wooden fortress on the Gosport side of the harbour began to roar again across the harbour and this time some real damage was done. The record says "Ours played soundly from Gosport and shot through the tower of the church (i.e. the Cathedral Church of St. Thomas's) and brake one of the bells, and shot again against the same tower and that rebounded and fell into the Church". The story goes on to say "the same Saturday morning they (the Gosport Gunners) shot at the Water-mill, the miller whereof commended it (by experience) for a good thing to rise early in the morning, for (as he said) if he had not risen early that morning, he had been killed in his bed, for a bullet took away a sheet and part of his bed". There is always a good excuse for getting up early on a Saturday.

The reason for shooting so much at the church tower was not any special objection to the church, but, as the contemporary chronicler says "for that at the top thereof was their watch-tower whereby they espied all the approaches by sea and land and the tolling of a bell gave notice both what ships came by sea and what numbers of horse came by land".

The record may, of course, be one sided, since it was written by a supporter of the Parliamentarians, but it claims gleefully that the Gosport gunnery was far superior to that of Portsmouth. "That Saturday night, ours shot but five bullets from Gosport, but every one of them did execution. It was well observed, that in a small time, as ours shot from Gosport, beginning at 4 of the clock on Friday afternoon and ending at 4 on the Sabbath-day in the morning, we did more execution with our two pieces of Ordnance, than the Governor with the Town Ordnance in 14 or 16 days and so many nights, in which they shot at least 300 bullets and killed but one man in all that time, a more remarkable providence of the Lord, we having but two pieces of Ordnance at Gosport, whereas the Ordnance planted against Gosport from their four works could not be less than 30 pieces of Ordnance". Perhaps it's not the only time that Gosport has stood up to its rival over the harbour with odds as great.

The next day, on the 29th August, 1642, there was more firing across the harbour when the Royalists returned to the attack, but the recorder says contemptuously, that their gunners "only made some holes into the tops of houses at Gosport, but killed neither a man nor horse". This was the day that the Town Clerk of Portsmouth was caught and imprisoned. Portsmouth was coming under heavier attack from all sides. On the 2nd September the guns of Gosport opened fire again and the Castle was attacked. More guns were mounted on the Gosport side of the harbour and a ten gun battery was established. Portsmouth surrendered to the forces of Parliament and Lord Goring left the town. It is said that he threw the town key into the harbour.

Troubles died down for a time in this area but it isn't quite the end of the story of Gosport and Lord Goring or of Gosport and the Civil War. Two and a half years later, in 1645, when the war was drawing to its close, Lord Goring raided the west country carrying the King's standard but also bringing destruction and death to many towns. Soon he was able to establish his headquarters near Romsey and was in command of both Winchester and Salisbury. His marauding raids carried him far afield. It was on the 6th January, 1645 and at about 6 p.m. that Goring's forces suddenly raided Gosport. They tore down the entrance gates and set fire to 24 houses. What made it even worse for the local inhabitants was that the Parliamentary ships in the harbour, the "Swiftsure" (260 tons) the "Mary Rose" (320 tons) and the "Fellowship" (400 tons) "shot divers pieces of Ordnance into them". Goring's men got away, but Gosport suffered even more damage. The record says that after the devastation of Gosport, "Goring marched westward driving off all the cattle, horses, sheep, swine, and carrying away men out of the Hundreds of Alverstoke, Fareham and Titchfield".

There are two final comments. It was declared that "one of the Cavaliers, who was chief in firing the houses, caught a gentleman of the town wearing two rings on his fingers, and being pressed for time, the wretched fellow cut off both his fingers to gain posession of the rings". The other comment is that when the King came into his own again, Portsmouth received a Charter, which gave the city control of Gosport. The charter lasted only a few years. There may not have been much value in it for we read that in 1647 the whole parish of Gosport was valued at £6. 4s. 8d. yearly.

The year 1664 was a troublesome one, not only because of the shocking state of politics. Plague struck with devastating effect and during that year the townsmen of Gosport fled to the village of Forton and lived in barns and huts while the plague caused misery and death in the town.

CHAPTER 4

Gosport and Alverstoke
during the early 18th century

Suppose you had been living in Gosport in 1760, just over 200 years ago, and had invited your friend to cross the harbour from Portsmouth to visit you. What would you have shown him and what would have been his impressions of the little town? As he scrambled from the ferry boat and up the muddy slipway, would he have been more favourably impressed than now? There would have been some evidence of decay, as today; but a good deal more of expansion. A small town, with two main streets and a large number of crowded alleyways with overhanging timber houses, cobbled streets with few pavements, dirty and dark by modern standards but with an air of liveliness, would have greeted him.

As your guest arrived at the sloping, slimy cobbled way leading from the harbour, he would have asked about the fort immediately to your north. It was Charles Fort and it stood on the site now occupied by Messrs. Camper & Nicholson. It had been erected nearly 100 years previously during the reign of Charles II but had never been very useful and was already in a state of decay. There was a small square tower made of stone about 4 feet thick with bastions on which were a few cannon. Around the fort was an earthen wall and a moat (or rather a dry ditch) about 10 feet deep and 10 feet across. A small earthwork protected the moat. The fort itself would not have been of much use against the French invader. Already in August 1698 there were complaints that it was delapidated and the doors needed repair.

This is the way in which Stephen Leake of the Navy Office described the defences of Gosport in 1729. "On the opposite side of this narrow water is another fort with a row of large cannon and a house and barracks strongly guarded by an old Irish gunner and four or five invalids—and no such thing as ammunition (except bread, cheese, small beer and gin) has appeared there for many years. The chief use it is put to is to accommodate the ladies who come there for the benefit of the fresh sea breezes or as a place of retirement to recover from a broken constitution". Charles Fort was not more warlike. By 1778 the fort had in fact become a public house and Thomas Morgan was granted rights to sell beer, etc. in Charles Fort, paying 10/- a year for the privilege. In September 1782 the fort was offered on lease for 7, 14, or 21 years as "all that building or tenement situated on the beach at Gosport, known by the name of Charles Fort, now and of late years used as a publick house". Replies had to be sent in by Wednesday, 2nd October. Mr. Whitcomb offered £205 per annum and was granted the lease. There was a considerable dispute about the extent of the property covered by the lease and some sheds belonging to other owners. Finally Mr. Whitcomb got a reduction in rent to £110. By 1838 it was in ruins and hidden by the Castle Tavern. Ultimately it was demolished to make retaining walls and roadways.

There was also another fort on Borough, Barrow, or Burrow Island at the entrance to Forton Creek. It was known as Borough Castle and later as James's Fort. There is a complaint dated 1698 which refers to the need for repairing the drawbridge which linked it with the mainland. The island on which it stood (until it was demolished in 1837) was the burial ground for convicts and prisoners of war in the Forton Hulks—it became known as Rat Island.

Opposite the fort you would have pointed out the town "Green"— Gosport Green where the spring and autumn fairs were held and around which were the homes of some of the wealthier inhabitants. Then you would have gone up the main street—Middle Street as it was then called. The number of small beer houses each having its own special brews of beer would have caused no special interest because it was typical of a small naval town. You would have noticed the India Arms since it was the largest and most dignified of the beer houses with capacious stabling at the rear. Middle Street would have impressed your friend as the residential centre of the chief townsfolk. In the main street almost opposite the India Arms was the Market House. Typical of the construction of such civic centres of the time it stood on stilts with room for market stalls underneath. It was an unattractive building, consisting as it did of a wooden shed with two small rooms in which the Lord of the Manor held his courts. The proprietor of the Market House was the Bishop of Winchester. The edifice remained until 1812 when it was pulled down. It had a small octagonal tower with a clock.

Going further up Middle Street with your friend you would have reached the main centre of the town where the High Street (Upper High Street and Lower High Street) crossed the main road. Close by was the chapel of the dissenters (now part of the United Reform Church). The record of the Dissenters in Gosport is unique. A group must have been established before the Act of Uniformity of 1662. But their church dates back to 1663 and is associated with Walter Marshall

(1628-1680). Marshall was ejected from his living at Hursley for his puritan convictions and by 1672 was established in Gosport. A meeting house was built in Lower South Street in the early 1690's. A parsonage, the gift of a lady of the sect, was purchased in Upper High Street. You might have seen the old theatre which stood on the site where the Congregational Church was erected in 1794 and remained until its destruction in 1941 during the Second World War. Still journeying a little further up the Middle Street, you and your friend would have seen evidence of the dangers of war, for Gosport was becoming a walled town. Ramparts running round the town to save it from attack were built in 1746 and 1758 and would have been shown as one of the new features of the town.

Retracing your steps down Middle Street you would certainly have taken your friend down Bemisters Lane, at this time used for carts as well as pedestrians, a narrow, crowded, residential thoroughfare, and would have come to Gosport Common. You would have noticed some fairly new almshouses which had been erected in 1693 by Lambert Peachy. The alms houses were for aged people. Two were built in 1693 for £50. Later eight more were added. Then you would have seen the new and imposing Trinity Church.

The idea of establishing a church in the heart of the growing town of Gosport came in 1694 when a group of local merchants and local business men—led by Captain Henry Player—determined to acquire a site of wild gorse and common land near the harbour's edge known as Gosport Common. Sanction was obtained from the Rector of Alverstoke (Reverend John Hunt) and from the Bishop of Winchester, Peter Mews. He contributed by sending by oxencart 14 oak trees from his estate at Farnham. These were to be used as pillars. The foundation stone was laid in September 1694 and after two years of building the consecration of the new church took place on 24th September, 1696. The records of the church are fairly complete and a delightful historical study of them was produced in 1954 by Mrs. Catherine Barclay (wife of the vicar). The Vestry Book records the Act of Consecration.

"Whereas Henry Player, Gent, and other the inhabitants of the Burro of Gosport in the County of Southampton have, at their own proper cost, and by the contributions of other pious and charitable Christians, upon a pious and religious account built, set up and finished this Chapel, in a waste piece of ground called Gosport Common, within the parish and the Liberties of the parish Church of Alverstoke in the County aforesaid, and in the jurisdiction of our Diocese of Winton, containing within the walls of it in length from East to West, the space of seventy and five feet and in breadth from North to South fifty and five feet or thereabouts, and have adorned the same with a Communion Table, handsomely furnished, with a Font, a Pulpit and convenient seats as well below in the space as in the Gallery above, and all other necessaries for the decent performance of Divine Worship, and have besought us, that by our Episcopal Authority on behalf of ourselves and Successors, would be pleased to separate the said Chapel from all profane and common uses, and dedicate the same for sacred and Divine Service, We, Peter, by Divine Permission, Bishop of Winton yielding to the pious and religious request as well of the said Henry Player, as of other inhabitants of the said Burro, do by our Episcopal Authority proceed to the Consecration of this Chapel built and beautifyed as before mentioned, and do separate the said Chapel, for ever, from all prophane and common uses, and devote, appoint and do Dedicate it for Divine worship and service only". A waste piece of land around was consecrated "for a Yard or Burying place, for the interring the Bodies of persons deceasing after a Christian manner". The infant son of Captain Henry Player and his wife Joanna was christened in the new church on 27th September, 1696.

By 1730 the church was in need of repairs and a collection made during April realised £121 10s. 0d. produced by 198 contributors. Thomas Bemister gave £8 8s. 0d. and Widow Palmer 1/-. Colonel Richard Norton of Southwick House gave £200. The Chapel was fully repaired and adorned. The next year a portico was added. The gift of the living was with the Rector of Alverstoke who was given "full and free power from time to time of naming a fit Minister to perform Divine Service". In 1730 the Rector appointed his own son—Dr. Charles Monckton.

The accounts of the Churchwardens show the variety of items with which they were concerned.

		s.	d.
1735	For mending the surplices to Goody Bastard	3	0
	For pens and ink to the Vestry 6 and Greenboughs at Easter	1	6
	For a Chamber pot to D		5
	For stuff and work, nails etc. to make the south gate	3	0
	For cutting down the weeds in the Chap-yard to Goody Bartholomew	1	0
	For candles, 3 months at 1/6 a time	4	6

In 1738 the expenses for the upkeep of the church were put at £23 6s. 8½d. including "2/6 for Candles, 8/6 for mending surplices and for making a blank book for raising money by gifts 2/-".

In 1745, following a dispute about reserving pews and paying pew rents, a letter was addressed to the bishop asking that the church should be enlarged at the eastern end. He wrote "The Town and Chappelry are becoming so populour that many of the Inhabitants for want of Convenient Seatroom cannott attend Divine Service in the said Chappel and that an Enlargement and Addition might be built and added to the East End of the said Chappel whereby about sixty convenient seats or pews may be added to the use of such of the Inhabitants as shall want and stand in need of convenient Seatroom". It cost £289 to carry out the alterations.

In 1748 the organ in the private chapel of the Duke of Chandos was sold to Holy Trinity for £117 12s. 0d. Actually the parishioners had to find much more than that sum to meet the cost of transport, repair and assembly. In the church records it reads "Item, an organ purchased from the Duke of Chandos's Chapel at Cannons, near London, by the subscription of the inhabitants. Cost and charges £341 16s. 7d. Opened the 8th May, 1748". The acccounts for this transaction are of particular interest. On the Duke's side it reads.

	£	s.	d.
To cash paid to Mr. Ch. Cock (the auctioneer) for organ as it stood at Cannons	117	12	0
Paid Mr. Jordan for taking it down and carriage to London	16	8	0
Paid Mr. Jordan for repairs	105	0	0
Paid Mr. Jordan for new swell	30	0	0
Paid Mr. Jordan for repairs and carriage to Gosport	8	0	0
Paid Mr. Richard Mullins for painting the organ	1	14	0

The Vestry Book of records include

To cash paid to Mr. Ch. Cock for the organ as it stood at Cannons	117	12	0
To Mr. Alan Jordan for taking it down from the chapel at Cannons, packing and bringing to London	16	8	0
To Mr. Alan Jordan for repairs	105	0	0
To Mr. Alan Jordan for addition of a swell	30	0	0
To Mr. Alan Jordan for repacking it for Gosport	5	0	0
To Mr. Chase for carriage	15	15	0

It is almost certainly true that the great composer Handel played on this instrument. Handel was the Duke's chapel master and director of music.

Subscribers to the organ fund were given the opportunity to hear two candidates play on the instrument for the post of official organist, the issue to be decided by popular vote. Mr. Moses Hawker of Portsmouth got 28 votes, but Mr. James Peaceable of Southampton got 141 and was duly appointed, a posi-tion he held for 11 years.

Just beyond the Church of the Holy Trinity and out past Haslar

Gate, your friend would have been greatly interested in a vast new building as yet unfinished across the narrow Haslar Lake and standing a little way from Fort Blockhouse. Ferrying across, for there was no permanent bridge, you would have seen a large number of builders at work on the new naval hospital to the design of the architect Theodore Jacobsen. It had been started in 1746 and would not be finished until 1762. Had you managed to get hold of a copy of "The Gentleman's Magazine" for September, 1751, you would have seen a drawing of the scheme. Originally it had been intended to build the hospital in the shape of a perfect square but the plan had later been modified. You would have told your friend that before the new hospital had been started the site was occupied by a farmhouse called Hazelwood and that there had been a windmill and a little woodland in the vicinity. But Jacobsen, the architect, had altered all this. Haslar was not of course, the first naval hospital in Gosport—there had been an earlier one built by Nathanial Jackson called the Fortune Hospital. It was near where the Detention Barracks stood. Jackson contracted to look after the sick and wounded sailors and the Board of Admiralty supplied him with 700 beds.

One surgeon described his work at Fortune Hospital thus

"My pay was five shillings a day constant and threepence for each man for medicine. I had also half-a-crown a day for each mate and a mate for every thirty men, so I had sometimes four mates' pay and but one mate in being. The three pence per man seemed worst but considering that many ran away as soon as they came, that most others were scurvy which costs little, the three pence per man did well enough though it was a small reward".

The Fortune Hospital had been built in 1713 and lasted under Jackson's direction until the 1720's. After his death there was a legal case in which his widow claimed that the 700 beds, all the other furniture and effects of the Fortune Hospital were household articles and were left to her in accordance with the marriage agreement. The courts decided otherwise—that the furniture was used in his business as contractor to the Commissioners for the Sick and Hurt. Jackson, it appeared, had not himself resided at the hospital and had no apartment there, leaving the task of looking after the wounded seamen to his servants.

The scandals associated with the contracting system are described in Lloyd and Coulter's monumental volume on Medicine and the Navy, Volume 3. In 1741 the Admiralty referred to the Commissioners for the Sick and Hurt the question of setting up naval hospitals. The Commissioners declared "We are persuaded that so great savings in point of expense would arise as might justly warrant the undertaking". "Nothing can be a greater motive to people voluntarily entering the service and continuing in it with cheerfulness than a thorough persuasion that whenever it happens to be their misfortune to be sick or hurt all proper tenderness and care will be used in their recovery".

A few years later, in 1744, there was an inquiry into the conditon of sick seamen in Gosport. It was asserted that "the want of Royal Hospitals is the cause of the lodgings, diet and nursing of sick men being performed by contract—a method liable to such abuses as are often fatal to the health of the seamen notwithstanding all the care taken to prevent it". "But when the folly of the poor men is considered in intoxicating themselves with strong liquors in the height of their distempers, the great numbers that are swept away by such intemperance, and the desertion of great numbers that recover, both compassion to them, and the interest of Your Majesty's Service requires the putting a speedy stop to of an evil of such pernicious consequences which can in no way effectively be done but by building hospitals".

But although the order for the building of the hospital was made on 7th November, 1744, work didn't start until two years later and it wasn't until 10th October, 1753, that the first section was opened for patients.

Haslar was built in red bricks made from local clay. It was a massive edifice, reputed to be the largest brick building in Europe. By 1761 the construction was completed and within 25 years more than 1880 patients were accommodated in 84 general medical and surgical wards. So great was the pressure on accommodation that Forton prison was used in 1779 as an overflow.

Lloyd and Coulter describe the Instructions laid down for the conduct of affairs within the Hospital. The job of Mr. T. Johnson, the Porter, who had been personally recommended for the post by Admiral Hawke, was "to warn off beggars, but be civil to strangers". To the Patients, the Instructions were, "Blaspheming, drinking, etc. or other scandalous action in derogation of God's honour and tending to the corruption of good manners to be fined. Not to quarrel or fight or leave the hospital or defile the place or sell drink or smoke except where permitted".

From May, 1758, until 1783 Dr. James Lind was Physician at Haslar at a salary of £200 a year. Haslar became the centre of the best medical research which earned Lind the title of the "Father of Nautical Medicine". Admiral Tait has described in his History of Haslar Hospital the problem of organising an enormous institution with inadequate staff and little conception of administration. Mrs. Cooper, one of the nurses, was accused of "gross abuse" on the Assistant Dispenser, Mr. Parker. She called him a "saucy impertinent fellow". Mr. Parker accused the Steward of stealing the hospital butter. All the

39

staff complained of shortage of pay. There were complaints, too, of nurses stealing the money and jewellery of the patients. In March, 1759, Miss Elias Smith took "a silk handkerchief containing a pair of silver buckles, a pair of Bristol stone buckles, and 3/6 in silver from a seaman patient from the Royal Arm who died in hospital and was reported to have been in possession of nine thirty shilling pieces, one guinea and a half". One of the regulations for nurses hung in the wards read "That all nurses who disobeyed the matron's orders, get drunk, neglect their patients, quarrel or fight with other nurses or quarrel with the men or do not prudently or cautiously reveal to the Superior Officers of the house all irregularities committed by the patients in their wards (such as drinking, smoking tobacco in the wards, quarrelling, destroying the medicines, or stores, feigning complaints and neglecting their cure) be immediately discharged and a note made against their names on the books of the hospital that they never more be employed". Nurses were not to make a will for any patient nor a nurse to accept a will made in her favour.

After a searching enquiry in 1795 the responsibility for the administration of the hospital passed from the medical side to a Governor. The hospital was, despite this, not a very happy place toward the end of the century. There were frequent desertions, sometimes 40 or 50 men would escape at a time, some of them to return later on roaring drunk. A favourite means was to get into the main drain and out into Haslar Creek. Men went out this way and gin came in by the reverse route.

Another feature of Gosport which you would have shown your friend on his visit in 1765 was what was later called Clarence Yard. Within the memory of people living in 1750 this had been a large private house adjacent to a furze covered common. It had an extensive garden and numerous wells. It had belonged to Captain Flyers. Later it was bought by the Countess of Clancarty who sold it to the government. It was then occupied by a Mr. Holmes, who was a contractor for supplying beer to the Navy. He erected several large brewing houses. But after 1750 there were rapid developments. In 1752 Messrs. Cummings and Shepherd of Gosport and Mr. Quick of Portsmouth installed new plant. The master brewer's house, originally a large barn, was considerably enlarged. In 1753 the creek was deepened and wharves of oak beams were constructed at a cost of £426. Between 1754 and 1757, six further new brewing houses were erected and new stores as well as a horse driven mill were established at a total cost of some £4,600. Indeed had we crossed the harbour on the 28th June, 1753, we should have seen the first consignment of coal being brought for unloading at the new harbour. Further additions were to be made during the next 25 years which made the Victualling Yard and

40

Naval Brewery (or as it was later to be called Royal Clarence Yard) an important Naval centre. But as with Haslar, Clarence Yard had in 1758 its greatest years of development in front of it.

As our friend returned after his visit to Gosport he would probably have gained the impression of a small, somewhat dirty but busy sea-town growing in importance and in size as a naval centre.

Meanwhile we can turn from the busy life of the growing town of Gosport, with its new crowded church, its merchants and traders, looking more and more to the harbour and the navy for its livelihood and becoming centred within the ramparts that had been built to enclose it, to the more rural life of Alverstoke some three miles away. This was the parish centre where the parochial officers were annually elected at the Easter Vestry. Here again it is upon the church records that we have to rely. There are registers of St. Mary's, Alverstoke, dated back to 1559 although of course the church itself (not the present building) can be traced back certainly to Norman and possibly Saxon times. The Vestry Books have entries from 1699. One entry dated 1711 is of particular interest because it suggests that important historic records were lost later on. The entry gives a list of the valuable property of the church. "One large silver flagon with Captain Player's coat of arms engraved on it; one chalice and cover, the gift of John Eames to the church; two silver plates with a cypher engraved on back; one old fashioned silver bowle; one tin box with charters of this parish therein and the manumission of Freedom". Now it is this tin box which is priceless—but unfortunately it was lost and there is no entry of it subsequent to 1800. The tin box, its key and its contents would go far to confirm or amplify our knowledge of the town.

The value of the church Vestry Books is enormous. During the 18th century the Parish was the centre not only of ecclesiastical life but of local government itself. It was at the annual vestry meeting that the chief (unpaid) officers of the civic life of the parish were selected and the main business of local government was transacted. Frequently, as at Alverstoke, church and civil items were inter-mixed. Much of the local government problem was concerned with the maintenance of the poor, orphans, aged, sick, widows, who were residents in the parish and were its liability. There was no national provision, the poor were dependent upon charity and the parish. Overseers of the poor were appointed annually to see that some provision was made, often at the least possible cost. The problem of poverty looms large in the Vestry Books. It was usual, for example, for parish children, the orphans and other destitute children to be apprenticed to local tradesmen. We read that in 1702 Mr. William Manfold decided that he would prefer to make a payment to the parish of £8 in order to be relieved of the obligation of having a parish child put to him. Sometimes older people were concerned, able bodied poor persons who could be set to work. So we read in 1725 "For the better employment and setting of the poor to work, a workhouse should be established in the parish. That the parish houses in South Street be rendered fit and useful for a workhouse for lodging and entertaining the said poor of this parish. That John Maynard be appointed master, at a salary of £20 a year and employ the poor in the woollen manufactory or some branches of it". But either the workhouse didn't pay (usually it didn't) or there was one of those economy drives, with which we are familiar today, for we read in 1733 in the Vestry Book, "That the salary or yearly pension of £10 and no more (exclusive of house room and maintenance) be allowed to any master of the workhouse belonging to this Parish".

Another way of meeting the problem of poverty among the young was to provide some very elementary kind of education and we find an entry dated 11th August 1711 which states "A piece of land belonging to the parish was granted for the building of a schoo. and a school house on the south side of South Street". Occasionally dire poverty resulted from sickness and the parish had to meet the cost of treatment. Thus in 1734 the record reads "It is ordered that 10 guineas be paid to Mr. Argent Blundell for the care he made of the fractured legs of William Dicker of this Parish."

But it wasn't only the deserving poor that had to be educated, apprenticed, cured, maintained or set to work. There were also the undeserving poor, the rogues and vagabonds. Thus on 21st January 1702 there is the following entry, "It is unanimously agreed that there shall be a new large cage for the security of rogues, vagabonds and other bold and unruly persons, and that the same ought to be built at the charge of the whole parish, and that the constables do take care to get the same sufficiently done and be reimbursed for the charges thereof by a parish rate". Or it might be that a new pound had to be erected. The record for 4th November 1720 reads "The pound for this liberty and Parish of Alverstoke was set up and finished, the timber being given by the Bishop of Winchester as Lord of the Manor". In 1750 the Vestry Records report that a fire engine was purchased by the inhabitants of Gosport by subscription.

All these civil duties were intermingled with church responsibilities. In 1724 the Vestry Records show that £20 7s. 4d. was spent on repairing the tower and it was stated that "the roof of the Parish Church should be taken off and a new roof made and covered with tiles, and that the outside walls of the said church should be raised five feet higher and the inside pillars thereof should also be raised and augmented proportionately". In 1725 we read "Rebuilding the Parish Church £212 3s. 10d. paid by Church Rate, non-payers to be prosecuted". The same job in 1957 cost £6,000 which amount had to be raised by voluntary subscriptions! The work didn't last long for in 1736 we learn the tower was very much decayed, the frames on which the bells depend are in danger of falling" and 1763 "The great bell being cracked it is thought that two smaller ones will be sufficient the big bell to hang useless".

Another valuable sidelight of local government in the 18th century is an astonishing entry in 1734. Whilst the parish was responsible for most local government services, such as they were, the County Quarter Sessions was the body that dealt with prisoners and bridges, but the parishes were ordered to meet their share of the cost. The record states "That forasmuch as the inhabitants of this parish are indebted and stand charged with several years Arrearages to County Stock, to wit from the year 1728, for Vagrant, Bridge money and Quarteridge money, amounting to £17 17s. 0d. or thereabouts, for which the Treasurer of the County of Southampton threatens to prosecute, it is therefore agreed that the money be paid out of the collections for the poor, for preventing further trouble and expense".

The accounts of the Churchwardens of Alverstoke for this period show the rural side of its life

		£	s.	d.
1744	May 16th. Paid to Richard Prignall for 4 foxes heads		4	0
	June 7th. 4 dozen sparrows heads			8
	July 3rd. Paid to Thomas Cocker for a hedgehog			4
	Sept. 21st For 9 dozen sparrows heads		1	6
1746	Paid Robert Taylor for 5 foxes heads		5	0
	Paid Philip Rickman for 12 dozen sparrows heads		2	0
	Paid George Wroat for burying two men at Gilkicker		2	0
	Paid Thomas Bowen for burying a man on the shore		1	0
	Paid attending the Justices at Fareham about some horned cattle		2	6
1748	May 13th. To a pole cat			6
	Jan. 1st To Wm. Hack for a stoat			4
1757	paid for badger		1	0
1761	April 20th paid James Churcher for 3 foxes' heads		3	0
1765	paid John Seagon for a wheel and hanging the new bells	2	15	0

But it wasn't only church affairs that were decided at Easter Vestry, or matters of local government like the poor law, or the stocks for the wrongdoers and vagrants. The people of Alverstoke had a sense of local ownership. In 1750 a special meeting of the Vestry was called "to take into consideration proper ways and means for the obtaining of satisfaction for certain casks of beef and pork unlawfully landed on the Jetty Head adjoining Mr. Carver's Key (quay) on Gosport beach, and forfeited to this parish, which the parish officers of Portsmouth have claimed and taken, to the prejudice of this parish". And they decided to seek legal advice.

They also kept a record of the boundaries of the parish by the time honoured custom of beating the bounds, more perhaps in good humour than to maintain legal rights. The Churchwardens Accounts include

		s.	d.
1748 Jan. 1st	Whipping boys at bounds	1	6
1752 April 10th	Paid for wands and painting in order to ride the bounds	6	0
	For beer at setting out	3	0
	For bread, beer and cheese at Stoke	13	0
	To a boy that was whipped	1	0
	To a boy that went through Gamur Pond	1	0
	To victuals and beer at the Town for the boys	17	3

Not that the Churchwardens could get away with extravagance. In 1765 an objection was lodged against one of the Churchwarden's accounts because he gave 3½d. a lb. for mutton and 3d. a lb. for beef in large quantities.

But even rural affairs suffer occasional shocks. It is recorded in Chamberlain's History and Survey of London and Westminster (1770) that "on the 18th March 1751 between five and six o'clock in the evening a shock of an earthquake was felt at Gosport, Portsmouth and the Isle of Wight which greatly alarmed and terrified the inhabitants. Several other places in Europe, particularly France and Germany, were visited with this dreadful calamity".

CHAPTER 5

Gosport's First Council

It was during the eighteenth century and the long period of the French wars that Gosport began to change from a small village to a sizeable town. In some ways the change was not for the better. The description given by The Reverend Dr. James Bennett in 1777 is probably an extravagant one, but it shows something of the conditions. "The town contains 5,000 inhabitants", says the worthy doctor, "and is opposite to Portsmouth. Except for the vicinity of the sea, Gosport can claim little that is attractive; for the town is not pleasant and the surrounding country has no peculiar charms. The town has the narrowness and slander of a small country town, without its rural simplicity and with a full share of the vices of Portsmouth, polluted by the fortunes of sailors and the extravagances of harlots. To these evils are added the petty pride and sectarian bigotry of a fortified town".

Not a pretty picture but it is one that is largely endorsed by an Act of Parliament of 1763. It was first introduced into Parliament on 19th May 1761. The act is entitled "For the better paving of the streets and for preventing nuisances and other annoyances in the Town of Gosport, in the County of Southampton". The preamble to the Act gives an excellent account of the condition of the town. "Whereas the Town or Borough of Gosport, in the Parish of Alverstoke and County of Southampton is not only large and populous, but has two Fairs annually and a market three times in every week kept therein, and is a place of great resort, being contiguous and adjoining to Portsmouth Harbour, in the said County; where not only the greatest part of Her Majesty's Navy, but a great number of merchant ships usually rendezvous; and whereas the streets in Gosport aforesaid, are chiefly paved, but most of such pavements are in a very bad and ruinous condition, the said Town is rendered unwholesome and dangerous, from the many nuisances and annoyances therein; and it has been found impracticable to keep the said streets in repair and to prevent such nuisances and annoyances by the present methods provided by law".

The Act appointed a number of persons as Commissioners for the purpose of putting "into execution all the powers and authorities in and by this Act given". They were Salter Andrews (Surgeon), William Attwick (Esquire), John Barham (Gentleman), John Barker (Gentleman), Charles Bedford (Brazier), William Bedford (Gentleman), Thomas Bishop (Esquire), Thomas Burges (Watchmaker), William Buckland (Gentleman), Erasmus Carver (Merchant), James Collins (Gentleman), William Cummings (Master House Carpenter), Thomas Curry (Merchant), William Duckett (Junior Gentleman), William Farr (Doctor of Physick), Jonathan Faulkner (Esquire), John Ganet (Grocer), Stephen Gafelee (Surgeon), Benjamin Gay (Wine Merchant), John Golighty (Brewer), Holoway Gover (Stationer), James Grift (Glazier), James Hackman (Esquire), Edward Harper (Surgeon), James Hobbs (Esquire), William Jolliffe (Haberdasher of Hats), William Harrison Edward Knowles (Mercer), Henry Lys (Brewer), Thomas Leddell William Marsh (Esquire—a Rear Admiral in His Majesty's Navy), Hide Mathis (Gentleman), John Missing (Esquire), Joseph Murray (Broker), Samuel Norris (Master House Carpenter), Christopher Navil James Oades (Apothecary), William Peachey (Esquire), John Penfold (Mercer), William Pike (Esquire), Richard Porter (Esquire), Sir Thomas Ridge (Knight), John Sketcheley (Gentleman), Jeremiah Tichler (Gentleman), Philip Ticher (Grocer), Joseph Villain (Grocer), Robert Waller (Surgeon), James Ward (Esquire), and Thomas Walter. They, and their successors, were to form the Commission or the Council. The variety of occupations and the large number of members, some 50 in all, shows that Gosport at the time was beginning to be of considerable size and importance.

What were the powers under the Act? It was declared that if any person should "throw, cast or lay any timber, bricks, stones, slates, clay, straw, wood, faggots, coals, boards, tubs, casks, or goods of any kind, into any open street or lane or passage within the said Town, and shall not take and carry away the same . . . within four hours next after the same shall be so placed therein, and before dark, every such person so offending, shall for every such offence, forfeit and pay the sum of ten shillings".

Further: "if any person shall cast, throw, set or lay any coal ashes, woodashes, rubbish, dirt, dung, filth or other nuisance whatsoever into any open street, lane or public passage within the Town, or hoop, cleanse, wash or scald any cask, or saw any stone or timber in any of the streets, every such person shall pay ten shillings for every day the nuisance is permitted to continue".

Then there was a special clause about Bemister's Lane. It said that for preserving the pavement as much as may be, and preventing inconveniences to passengers passing through Bemister's Lane leading out of Middle Street (now High Street) into South Street to the Chapel and Meeting house, the Trustees might set up cross bars at each end of the lane and keep them locked, delivering a key to the occupier of any house in the said lane. The said lane, Bemister's Lane, was described as being "not broad enough for carts and foot-passengers at the same time to pass and repass". There was a fine of ten shillings for driving a cart down the lane.

This Act was not very effective and afterwards a further Act was passed with the object of "Amending and Rendering more effective the former Act". The Trustees were now given power to arrange for the streets to be lighted properly, to set up a nightly watch, to order dangerous swinging signboards to be taken down, to see that the names of streets were affixed and to arrange for houses to be numbered.

It was on the 19th May, 1763, that twenty of the Trustees assembled at the India Arms in Middle Street. We have a copy of their signatures at the first meeting. There was William Farr, the doctor of physick, Philip Richer a grocer, William Cummings a carpenter, John Golightly a brewer and sixteen others. They found that only three streets were properly paved. They decided to appoint a night watchman and they determined to stamp out the practice of slaughtering animals in the open roadway. Carts were not to be allowed to have narrow wheels that made deep ruts, but wheels of at least four inches of iron in width. But the streets were still of pebbles and there were no gutters. After the first flourish of reforming zeal the Trustees ceased to exercise their duties effectively and by 1800 conditions were as bad as ever.

1. Horse tram at the Harbour. This photograph of about 1908 shows the ferry and floating bridge with H.M.S. St Vincent moored off Fort Blockhouse.

2.   An alley off the High Street.

MARTIN SNAPE. WATERCOLOUR C 1920. GOSPORT MUSEUM COLLECTION.

3.   Beach Street.

MARTIN SNAPE. WATERCOLOUR C 1920—GOSPORT MUSEUM COLLECTION

4. Anglesey Road looking south with Alverstoke Church on the right. To the left the Old Rectory.

MARTIN SNAPE. WATERCOLOUR C 1890 GOSPORT MUSEUM COLLECTION.

5. Fair on the Green.

MARTIN SNAPE. WATERCOLOUR C 1910 GOSPORT MUSEUM COLLECTION.

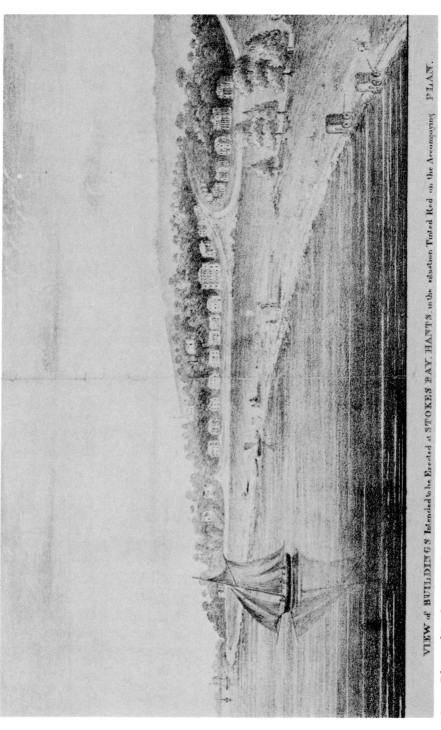

VIEW of BUILDINGS Intended to be Erected at STOKES BAY, HANTS, in the situation Tinted Red on the Accompanying PLAN.

GOSPORT MUSEUM COLLECTION.

6.   Plan of Stokes Bay by an unknown artist. Early nineteenth century.

7. Evening scene at the Hard, showing the ferry landing stage with Camper and Nicholson's and Ratsey and Lapthorn's buildings. The Old Market House is just visible on the left.

8. Visit of Louis Phillipe, King of France and entourage to Royal Clarence Yard in October 1844.

TINTED ENGRAVING. ARTIST UNKNOWN. GOSPORT MUSEUM COLLECTION.

9. Queen Victoria and Prince Albert arriving at Gosport Railway Station in Spring Garden Lane in October 1844. The French King helps the Queen from her carriage.

TINTED ENGRAVING. ARTIST UNKNOWN. GOSPORT MUSEUM COLLECTION.

10. Ratsey and Lapthorn's sail-loft.

MARTIN SNAPE. WATERCOLOUR C 1910. GOSPORT MUSEUM COLLECTION.

11. Hardway Creek, looking towards Portsdown Hill and Portchester Castle.

MARTIN SNAPE. WATERCOLOUR C 1910. GOSPORT MUSEUM COLLECTION.

12. The original Market House in the High Street, then called Middle Street. It was pulled down in the early nineteenth century. The building to the left is the India Arms Inn, now premises of Lennards and Wooltons.

13.　Forton Creek, the spire of Forton Church to the right.　MARTIN SNAPE. OIL ON CANVAS. C1905. PRIVATE COLLECTION.

14.　Gosport landing stage and foreshore.

MARTIN SNAPE. OIL ON CANVAS. C 1910. GOSPORT TOWN HALL.

15.   Fleetlands House.

MARTIN SNAPE, WATERCOLOUR C 1915. PRIVATE COLLECTION.

16. A panoramic view of Haslar Hospital with Fort Blockhouse and Haslar Creek. Early nineteenth century engraving.

CHAPTER 6

Some Incidents in the Life of Gosport between 1760 and 1800

During the forty years from 1760 to 1800 England was rarely at peace. The Seven Years War broke out in 1756 and ended in 1763 with the Treaty of Paris. A few years later, in 1775, the American War of Independence began and not until 1783 was peace restored again. Then in 1793 came the Revolutionary Wars with France which lasted on and off until 1815.

During this long restless period, Portsmouth was both the centre of naval preparations and attack as well as the most dangerous spot for threatened invasion. The great wooden fighting ships were built at Lymington, fitted and victualled in the harbour and assembled for war at Spithead. Gosport was inevitably affected by these war-like preparations and its story through these years bears witness to the valour, and the treachery; the adventures and the alarms of the times. News of famous victories, dangers of threatened invasions, the herding of prisoners of war, the swift descent of the press gang, battered ships sailing into port with wounded and sick sailors, well trimmed ships of the line sailing out of the harbour, these were part of the life of Gosport.

It became by 1760 a defended town. Since the 1740–50 period, earth ramparts had been constructed from Blockhouse Point round the outskirts to Forton Creek. A plan of the town dated 1748 shows the new fortifications begun that year and the work yet to be carried out. The object was to prevent Gosport from being taken and used by an invading force to attack Portsmouth. Across the harbour mouth from Blockhouse Point to Sally Port was a great cumbersome chain which could be tightened to prevent enemy ships from raiding the harbour. In 1778, for the last time, the capstans at Blockhouse were turned and the huge chain stretched tight. It was a time of wild rumours and news had been received of a French fleet off Plymouth, sailing towards Portsmouth.

Prisoners of war lived their dreary lives in Gosport. The old Fortune Hospital, built in 1713 in the Forton area was used, after the building of Haslar Hospital, as a camp for French prisoners. But in 1755 we read that it was decided "that Portchester Castle was a better place for their reception than the premises of a certain Mr. Ward at Fortune, near Gosport". In 1777 during the time of the American War of Independence an Act of Parliament was passed to "empower His Majesty to secure and detain persons charged with or suspected of the crime of High Treason committed in any of His Majesty's colonies or plantations in America or on the High Seas, or the crime of Piracy". Later in 1777 in the "London Gazette" it was announced "The King has been pleased by warrants under the Royal Sign Manual, to appoint a certain messuage of building called Forton on the Gosport side of Portsmouth Harbour in the Parish of Alverstoke in the County of Southampton, to be a place of confinement of such prisoners". So the first Americans to come to Gosport came as prisoners of war, to be lodged at Forton.

Technically they were regarded not as prisoners of war but Englishmen guilty of High Treason. In 1778, 57 of them determined to escape. They found an old cellar and began to dig out the earth hiding the soil in their beds. They worked out a passage beyond the main wall of the prison and one by one crawled out to feedom. It was said that not one of them was ever recaptured. A reference to this escapade is given in "Portrait of my Mother" by Ann Bridge:

"But this is history, and as children we cared little for history as such. What we enjoyed enormously was to hear my mother relate, as she loved to do, and did very well, the story of 'your great, great grandfather Hinman's escape from prison at Portsmouth'. Forton Prison the books call it. Hinman, who was very free with his spelling refers to it as Fortin, in his list of "Expences" in connection with his escape—which list also lies before me on frail ribbed paper yellow with age, the bold handwriting standing out clearly. After mentioning that in May 1778 at St. Kits he payed £2 15s. 0d. for "yams, foules and sondres" and the same sum for fresh pork—in Barbados currency—as he carefully notes—come the sombre entry:

"Expences at Portsmouth from 7th July until the 14th for fresh meat, bread, butter, greens, chese, and Stra £5 5s. 0d. and Sondres at ditto from 14th July until we were landed for articles as above". The next item is more cheerful "Payed for 13 gallons of Rum whilst in prison at Fortin £5 0s. 8d.". The list continues

"Payed Sondre Expences for myself of macking my escape from prison, passing threw France to Brest

gave a soldier to let me pass	£4	4	0
gave an old woman to conceal me in her house	£5	5	0
expences on road to London for chase hire and sondres	£1	1	0
payed Mr. Jackson for frayting me to London	£5	0	5
payed Mrs. Bayley at London for concealing me	£1	1	0

payed Mrs. Hardy for ditto	£2	2	0
payed expences from London to Deal	£4	6	4
payed a botte to carry me to Duncarck	£5	5	0"

and he does the sum as £29 18s. 4d. the price of escape from incarceration to freedom.

A verse was composed about Forton which went

"And Forton's Keep, a dread abode
Where neath misfortune's heavy load
Ambition's slaves, for despot's crime
Were captive held in warlike Time".

Again during the Napoleonic wars, Forton was used to house French prisoners of war, both within the old wooden barracks and the stone central block as well as in the bulks moored in Forton Creek.

This grim side of life was also reflected in the gibbet which stood on Block house beach on which the bodies of local miscreants were hanged as a warning to evil doers, whether criminals or traitors. In 1777 James Hill (alias James Aitken) who was commonly known as Jack the Painter attempted to set fire to the dockyards at Plymouth and at Portsmouth. He was hanged at the Dockyard Gate. This was on the 10th March, 1777. The mast of the Arethusa was erected to its height of 64 feet just within the Dockyard Gate and Jack the Painter was hoisted to the top with a rope round his neck. His body was brought to Blockhouse and hanged in chains there on the gibbet. The story is told that some sailors in a drunken frolic took the skeleton of Jack and left it in a public house in Gosport as a pledge for payment for beer. The local poets made a song about the incident:—

Whose corpse by ponderous irons wrung
High upon Blockhouse Beach was hung,
And long to every tempest swung?
Why truly Jack the Painter.
Whose bones some year since taken down,
Were brought in curious bag to town;
And left in pledge for half-a-crown?
Why truly Jack the Painter.

This reminds us that in 1780 a criminal, named Bryan, was executed at Winchester and his body, dressed in a new black suit, new shoes and ruffles was hung on the gibbet at Blockhouse. There is also the story of David Tyrie who was caught as a traitor sending to the French particulars of naval preparations at Portsmouth. His body was hanged, drawn and quartered on Southsea Common but the mob scattered the guards and fought to get parts of the corpse. A man whose name was Adams and who was the master of the Prison (Bridewell) at Gosport obtained the head which he preserved in spirits and exhibited for some years.

There were some brighter sides to life, for in 1773 His Majesty George III came to Portsmouth and crossed to Gosport to visit the naval brewery at Weovil. He distributed £2,100 between the workers in the dockyard, the crew of the Royal Yacht and the poor of Portsmouth, Gosport and Portsea.

In many ways the most interesting person living in Gosport during the second half of the 18th century was the iron master Henry Cort, whose inventions of the puddling and rolling processes and the use of coal in iron smelting ushered in the industrial revolution in the iron industry.

Although he was born in Lancaster in 1740, Henry Cort worked in Gosport and Fareham from 1776 until his death, in penury and ignominy on 23rd May, 1800. Cort came to London at the age of 25 and was for about 10 years a Naval Agent, contracting for supplies for the Admiralty, with an office in the Strand. He became friendly with Samuel Jellicoe, the son of the Deputy Paymaster of Seamen's Wages.

In 1776 he gave up his business as a contractor to undertake experimental work in the iron trade and for this purpose he acquired a forge at 18a, The Green, Gosport, and at Fontley in Fareham. Here he worked in partnership with Samuel Jellicoe but with considerable financial backing from Samuel's father, Adam Jellicoe.

Many attempts had been made to produce iron without using wood or charcoal. Cort developed and improved on these early crude experiments and combined them into a single process. The secret of his method was to transfer the pig iron from the blast furnace into a second furnace called a reverberatory furnace which was heated by ordinary coal. In the door of the furnace there were openings through which, by means of long rakes, the workmen could push the bar–iron and thus stir or "puddle" the metal. After about an hour of this stirring process the iron was in huge lumps called "loops" and these were heated again and passed through huge rollers which squeezed out the dross. The effect of Cort's work was to consolidate the processes of puddling and rolling using coal in both cases, and open up the vast iron industry of the 19th century. The iron trade left the vicinity of the forests to settle on the coalfields of the Midlands, South Wales and Scotland.

Henry Cort's patents were taken out on 17th January, 1783, and 13th February, 1784. The first patent is described as a "peculiar method of preparing welding and working various sorts of iron and reducing the same into uses by machinery, a furnace and other apparatus adapted and applied to the same purpose". The second patent was designed to protect "a new mode of shingling, welding and manufacturing iron and steel into bars, plates, rods, and othewise of purer quality in large quantitites by a more effectual application of fires and machinery with a greater yield than any method before attained or put into practice".

The consequences of these inventions were astonishing. In the 1740 period the iron trade was a dying industry with a production of little over 17,000 tons a year. Within five years of Cort's patents it had reached 68,000 tons and by 1796 125,000 tons. By 1806 production was over 250,000 tons. Not only could the rich coal fields be used in conjunction with huge iron deposits but the iron could be produced much more quickly. Fifteen tons of bar iron could be obtained in the time previously necessary for one ton. And too the quality of the iron produced by the new process was greatly improved. The Navy Board made detailed tests and in 1787 decided to use iron produced by the Cort process instead of Swedish iron for the casting of anchors. Cort bought iron stone and also acquired old disused iron cannon and shells from the Admiralty. There is evidence of coal being brought to Gosport from the north-east coast from 1753 but the trade increased considerably with the local demand of the iron forge on The Green.

Cort's industry caused local opposition. The local Trustee Authority which had been established in 1763 threatened Cort with prosecution if he failed to get rid of the mounting deposits of clinkers. In 1779 they ordered him to appear at their next meeting to show cause why he should not be fined for suffering his men to carry out, lay and continue large quantities of coal ashes and cinders on The Green and the highway, he having had several notices to the contrary. After this the clinkers were carried to the foreshore to become the basis of what later was transformed into the Ferry Gardens.

It is doubtful whether Cort's work at Gosport would ever have developed into a major iron industry. His inventions made it desirable to site the industry where both iron and coal were in proximity. But Cort suffered financial disaster in his personal fortunes. To establish his partnership with Samuel Jellicoe he had borrowed heavily from Adam Jellicoe who was in fact, as Deputy Paymaster of Seamen's Wages, using Admiralty funds for the purpose. In fact Cort's capital to develop big inventions came largely from public sources. Cort had given his patents and handed over half his stock and profits to Adam Jellicoe as security. Adam Jellicoe died owing to the Admiralty funds about £27,000. Cort was held responsible and his patents were seized and his outstanding contracts taken over. Instead of the 10/- per ton licence fee from ironmasters using his process Cort got nothing.

Cort, whose "ingenious and meritorious improvements in the art of working and making iron" might have made his fame and fortune, was utterly overwhelmed financially and forced into bankruptcy. The Admiralty did practically nothing about the patents. An official report in 1805 said "as to the patents, it does not seem that any opportunity has occurred, though endeavours have been used, to make it available to any profitable purpose". The ironmasters took over his processes without making payments under the licences and Cort, in fact, received nothing for his inventions. Samuel Smiles in his Industrial Biography quotes James Watt as saying in 1784, "Mr. Cort has, as you observe, been most illiberally treated by the trade; they are ignorant brutes; but he exposed himself to it by showing the process before it was perfect, and seeing his ignorance of the common operations of making iron, laughed at him and despised him; yet they will contrive by some dirty evasion to use his process or such parts as they like, without acknowledging him in it".

As a result of a petition to Parliament, where he was decribed as 'the Father of the British iron trade', Cort received a state pension of £200 a year. But he had a family of 12 children and after his death in May 1823 the family fortunes suffered badly. In 1811 a collection was taken among the great ironmasters of the country to help relieve the family but it produced the sum of only £871 10s. 0d. The records of Holy Trinity Church reveal the declining fortunes of the family

Whether the major part of Cort's inventions were made at The Green at Gosport or at Funtley at Fareham is not known. But in 1854 when the Old Foundry at Gosport Green was being dismantled, a furnace was discovered which closely resembled the description of the original reverberatory furnace and may well have been the one in which Cort carried out his experiments. The black sand used in moulds was several feet in depth revealing how extensive the industry on The Green must have been.

CHAPTER 7

Gosport in 1791

Nothing reflects so well the life of a small town as its local newspaper. Hitherto in our story of Gosport we have had to rely upon scraps of information, parish records, deeds, act of parliament, etc. But by the 1780-90 period the newspaper begins to take its place as the chief means of record. The earliest newspaper I have seen for the Gosport district is the "Hampshire Chronicle and Portsmouth and Chichester Journal" for the year 1791.

Rather than retell its news of Gosport I am recording some of the news items and advertisements that appeared between January and June, 1791. They reveal something of what was going on in the town.

January 8th, 1791. "On Friday last in consequence of an unhappy dispute concerning the present state of politics a duel was fought on the beach in front of Haslar Hospital between a Mr. L. of Gosport and a lieutenant in the navy. After the exchange of a case of pistols each, the lieutenant unfortunately recieved a shot in his thigh which brought him to the ground. He was immediately carried to the house of a surgeon who seemed to think that amputation of the limb must ensue. As the wounded gentleman's life is supposed to be in danger, the seconds were immediately taken into custody. Mr. L. made his escape".

January 22nd. "A theatre is to be opened at Gosport by Mr. Thornton, formerly prompter to Mr. Webster's company at Portsmouth and we understand is likely to meet with encouragement".

January 31st. "Whereas Ann, the wife of Charles Cox of Brockhurst in the parish of Alverstoke has left me, and, as I am informed cohabits with another man, I hereby forbid all persons from trusting the said Ann Cox anything on my account".

February 12th. "Yesterday morning Lieutenant Wilkes opened a rendezvous at Gosport for entering seamen for His Majesty's fleet". Later, on March 26th, it was reported "At Lieutenant Wilkes' rendezvous at Gosport for volunteers, seamen enter very fast since the late proclamation offering a bounty and much commendation is due to that officer for his great exertions and unwearied attention to service".

February 12th. "Apprentice wanted to a baker in good business. Enquire of Mr. Henry Price, baker, or of Mr. William Harding, Stationer of Gosport. None need apply who cannot bring a good character". Later, on May 18th, another advertisement stated, "Wanted an apprentice to a baker and pastry cook. Letters post paid directed to Harding, booksellers, or William Ashford, baker, will be duly attended to. N.B. A handsome premium will be duly expected".

February 21st. "Deserted from H.M. company of Royal Military Artificers and Labourers stationed at Fort Monckton near Gosport on 8th February, 1791, William Clements aged 20 years; 5 feet 9½ inches; born at Hill Pond near Droxford; by occupation a labourer; is straight and well made, swarthy complexion, hazel eyes, brown hair and large eye brows; has lately had the small pox which nearly occasioned the loss of one eye and has very much marked the face. Whoever apprehends the said deserter will receive the reward allowed by Act of Parliament".

March 7th. "Priddy's Hard Magazine near Gosport. The respective officers of H.M. Ordnance at this place hereby give notice that on March 31st they will be willing to receive tenders for delivery of 380 chaldrons of the best Newcastle coals free of all charge or risk, into H.M. stores at the brick Kilns near Stokes Bay House".

March 26th. "The 30th regiment, lately returned from the West Indies have received orders to do duty at Forton Barracks".

"A French lady, said to be of considerable fortune (aged about 20) being a ward, and not able to procure the consent of her guardian, decamped from the continent with a French gentleman (aged about 25) and arrived one day last week at Gosport in order to be made happy at the altar of Hymen. On Friday last four French gentlemen relations to the lady, arrived in pursuit of them, by order of her guardian, and having found out the house where they were, went and focibly took the lady to the India Arms in the said town and locked her up with themselves in a room. However, by the contrivance of some Englishmen, she found means to escape with her lover and go off to London. A gentleman of Gosport has been committed to prison for assisting them in getting off".

April 16th. "A commodious bridge is shortly to be erected for carriages and foot passengers across the lake from Haslar Hospital to Gosport. Government having thought proper to grant to Mr. Robert Forbes, merchant of Gosport, liberty of building the same for which he is to have a certain toll and it being a considerable thoroughfare will be found more convenient than the usual mode of ferrying over". And in an earlier issue occurred the advertisement. "Contract. On Tuesday the 19th April tenders in writing will be received from such persons as may be inclinable, to contract for the building of a bridge of stone or

56

brick and timber across Stoke Lane from the Royal Hospital at Haslar to the Windmill opposite on the Gosport side".

April 13th. "Mr. Evans begs leave to return his most grateful acknowledgements for the very liberal encouragement he has already received of the gentlemen travellers who have hitherto been pleased to honour him with their company as also his numerous friends residing at Gosport and its vicinity and the public in general and takes the liberty of acquainting them that he is removed from the Bear, Cross Street, to the Dolphin Inn, which is conveniently situated at the entrance of the said town from London and Cross Roads—he has fitted up the same in a gential manner".

Both the news items and the advertisements in the "Hampshire Chronicle" for the second half of 1791 tell us interesting news of the life in the town.

Gosport was beginning to have a social life of its own and on 11th July an advertisement appeared for a new dancing academy. "Mr. Alliez, dancing master of the Royal Academy, begs leave to acquaint the ladies and gentlemen of Portsmouth and Gosport, that he has taken the Society Room, Old Rope Walk, Portsmouth Common; and the Coffee Room at the White Lion, Gosport, for the reception of such ladies and gentlemen as wish to be instructed in that polite art. Mr. A. having been engaged from Paris at the Royalty Theatre opened some years since and having taught the first nobility in London, therefore hopes for the favour of the gentlemen and ladies at the above places. His terms are Ten Shillings and Sixpence a quarter. His days of attendance Saturdays". We wonder how many of the well-to-do ladies of Gosport patronised the dancing master.

Another evidence of the growing size and importance of Gosport is revealed in an announcement in the paper of the 5th September concerning the formation of a Gosport Bank. "Opened on the 25th August 1791" it declares "for the accommodation of their friends and the public in general by Messrs. Thomas Curry and Thomas Curry Junior". "Every person keeping an account at this bank will be supplied with printed checks on which they may draw, either for money, or for our notes payable at sight, or for our drafts payable in London, at any date, without being charged for stamp". The announcement goes on to describe how persons without an account could get notes of the bank either for money or for good bills payable in London. Amounts of £100 or more were to be accepted and interest was to be paid at 3% per annum. The bank thus opened lasted for some years.

Yet a third indication that Gosport was developing came in an announcement made on 27th June—an announcement so astonishing that it reveals an attempt to make Gosport a cross-channel port. The whole advertisement is worth reproduction:

"Gosport and Harve de Grace Pacquet. A new Yacht the "Trotters', of sixty tons burden, a remarkable fast sailer, with elegant accommodation for passengers, is now established by P. Campbell, of Gosport, and kept constantly going between Portsmouth and Harve de Grace. She is adapted for carrying horses and carriages. Those who wish for a passage or to send goods are requested to apply to Mr. J. Dunlop, Merchant, White Friers, London, P. Campbell, general agent, Gosport who has convenient warehouses for receiving ship's cargoes. Letters or parcels addressed to the care of P. Campbell as above will meet with the strictest attention. This (although neglected for want of a regular good pacquet) is well known to be the most safe and speedy passage from London and the west of England to Paris and all the manufacturing towns of Normany; Gosport being 20 miles nearer Harve de Grace than Southampton and Harve de Grace 40 miles nearer Paris than Calais is". It appears that our forefathers in the 1790 period had ideas beyond those of today. The attempt to make Gosport a cross–channel port had its dangers f_r on 12th December we read in the news, "This week were seized and brought to the customs house at Gosport, nearly 200 kegs of spirit".

Another item of extraordinary interest appeared in the press on 5th December. It will be remembered that by 1790 the Industrial Revolution was beginning to affect the newish cotton industry of Lancashire and the new machines driven at first by swift flowing streams were being established in all the Lancashire valleys. To get the labour, pauper children were apprenticed and sent north in droves. Some of the worst horrors of the early industrial revolution arose from the employment of these young children in conditions that were close on slavery. It is significant to read "Last · veek three covered wagons in which were 49 boys and girls, were sent from the workhouse at Gosport, for Manchester, in order to be bound apprentices in cotton manufactories of that place. They appeared perfectly happy as well as healthy, and it were to be wished that parish officers in general were attentive to the placing out the children of indigent parents so as to render them useful members of the community". It is a comment that they were sent off in wagons during the first week in December.

Of all the many items that could be noted during the six months, the sales of houses, of coaches, of a horse and gig, of the request by a young lady for board and lodging, of the outcome of the notorious elopement from the India Arms, perhaps the advertisement for an Auction Sale on Thursday the 19th October at the India Arms at Gosport is the most interesting since it refers to many local places. The auctioneer was Thomas Ayling and there were 9 lots of property for disposal.

"Lot 1. All that farm known by the name of Holders situate on the south side of the turnpike road leading from Gosport to Fareham, and near the two mile stone consisting of a barn, 33 acres of arable land, and one acre of meadow, now in the occupation of John Page, tenant at will, at the yearly rent of £30.

Lot 2.   All that small farm consisting of a barn, garden, twenty two acres of arable land and two acres of coppice, situate at Elson near Gosport, now in the occupation of Jonathan Long, tenant at will at the yearly rent of £15.

Lot 3. All that small farm consisting of a farm house, barn, stable, gate room and thirty-six acres of arable land, situate at or near Stoke, within a mile and a half of Gosport, now in the occupation of James Ayling, tenant at will, at the yearly rent of £23.

Lot 4.   All that tenement with the garden and premises thereunto belonging, situate at Hardway, near Gosport, adjoining westwards to the public house known by the sign of the Blue Anchor, now in the occupation of James Mathews at the yearly rent of £5".

Space doesn't permit specifying all the lots, but Lot 6 is specially interesting.

"Lot 6.   All that tenement, or dwelling house and premises, being the corner house, situate at the lower end and on the north side of the North Street in Gosport, which now is, and for many years past hath been, a good and well accustomed grocer's shop, now in the occupation of Jol.n Burton Trimmings who holds the same on lease at the yearly rent of £30 in peace and £40 in war, for the term of 14 years, six of which have expired".

CHAPTER 8

Gosport during the Napoleonic Wars

During the long period of the Revolutionary and Napoleonic wars which lasted, almost without intermission from 1793 to 1815, Gosport was becoming increasingly important as a centre of naval activity. It was also growing rapidly as a town. At the end of the period there were about 2,000 houses and a total population of about 10,000. The town was much more congested than at present, for a very large proportion of the population was hemmed within the fortifications which had been erected some 50 years earlier.

The Ancient and Modern History of Portsmouth, Portsea, Gosport, and their environs says this of Gosport in 1801: "The approach by water is extremely fine, the different yards, the handsome ranges of houses on the beach, its ancient castle, the crowded quay, the range of barracks and the extensive building of Weevil; the whole bounded on the left by the entrance of the harbour, the Block-house, the Royal Hospital at Haslar and its lake, and on the right by the magazine, Forton Lake with the ancient castle at its entrance, present a prospect which we believe few could view without some emotion. Nor are the approaches from the land side less interesting. The London Road leads by Forton Prison and the new military hospital, along the foot of the works, occasionally enlivened by a glimpse of the lake . . . Another road, from Alverstoke and the adjacent country, far more private, passes the elegant hamlet of Berry so much adorned by the surrounding country . . . enters the town on the south west". "The town itself is handsome and populous, the principal street is Middle Street, which is broad and well built, extends westward from the harbour to the works, and is of a great length, and were it not for the obstruction of the market place, would be exceeded by few. Cold Harbour (later Clarence Square) is peculiarly fortunate in this respect; being open to the harbour, ornamented with several rows of trees and entirely the residence of private families; excepting at the occasional time of the military parade, affording an unusual scene of privacy and retirement. The circumstances of its having little or no connection with the more busy scenes of the town, and the advantage of a broad and extensive pavement on its southern side; with the agreeable addition of being occasionally enlivened by the charms of military music has caused it to become the usual resort for the evening promenade of the ladies and gentlemen of this town where the gay assemblage of beauty and fashion cannot but give a stranger the highest and most favourable ideas of the place".

About Alverstoke the writer became positively lyrical. "Thus we see this charming district not only amply endowed by the liberal hand of nature, richly interspersed with wood and lawn, with elegant commodious villas, farms and comfortable cottages, encircled with every species of cultivation from the garden to the cornfield, but amply secured by the hand of art—and from its highly favoured situation affording every advantage and every pleasure that can result from the vicinity of the scenes of business to the more agreeable and fascinating ones of rural retirement".

The returning sailors certainly didn't see Gosport in such a romantic light. A ballad of the time, taken from the Miscellaneous Works of Henry Mann and dated 1802 runs—to the tune of "A cobler there was"—

> I sing not of Naples, of Venice, of Rome,
>   Of the pillars of Trajan, or Peter's fine dome;
> Neither praise I old Brentford, that place of renown,
>   But will sing of a seaport and Gosport's the town.
>   Derry down etc.
> If the streets were more clean, you'd walk at your ease
>   But, believe me, the mud is quite up to your knees;
> Which, though not quite so pleasant as meadows and lawns,
>   Is convenient enough, since it's soft to the corns.
>   Derry down etc.
> For all those who're oblig'd to walk out in the night
>   Can't complain of the lamps, that they give a bad light,
> That the oil is too bad, or the wicks are too small,
>   I'll be curst if they can, for there's no light at all.
>   Derry down etc.
> And the inns are so noble, no neat, and so clean,
>   If you talk of a mop they scarce know what you mean,
> All infections, however, they keep from their doors,
>   With tobacco-juice sprinkled, to sweeten the floors.
>   Derry down etc.
> The want of fine buildings, and grand colonades,
>   Is made up by fine women, dear, good-humoured jades;
> Though the lasses of pleasure, take black, fair and brown,
>   Scarce amount to ten thousand in all Gosport town.
>   Derry down etc.

It was in Portsmouth Harbour and at Spithead that the great fleets were assembled for the naval campaigns that had their climax at Trafalgar in 1805, but it was from the Gosport side of the harbour that the victualling of the ships was organised, that supplies and armaments were stored. It was to the great Naval Hospital at Haslar that the sick and wounded were brought. It was in Gosport, too, that the Press gangs operated and many French prisoners were brought to the town.

These were exciting times, with tales of refugees from the French Revolution followed by wild rumours of a threatened invasion. There were deserters lurking in dark narrow alleys, there were dangers of riots from sailors who had returned from perilous adventures and were released temporarily from rigorous discipline. In addition there were stories of smugglers hiding their contraband goods in underground cellars.

After the September massacre in 1792 in France, aristocrats and priests were hounded out of the country. Gosport received its share of persecuted clergy. We read "The September massacre drove a large number of priests from France to the coast of Hampshire. They landed in the neighbourhood of Gosport and were hospitably received by the local clergy and residents". An address by 120 refugees written in elegant French and sent to Messieur John Sturges, Cure d'Alverstoke et Messieur I. M. Bingham, the "Ministre de la Chappelle de Gosport" expresses their gratitude for the sympathetic affection shown to them.

Stories of the Press gang abound in the narrow streets of Gosport. One of the most remarkable is that related in the Hampshire Telegraph in 1809. "There was a very hot Press on Tuesday night by which five hundred seamen were obtained. At ten o'clock at night Captain Bowers assembled a party of marines with as much noise as possible to quell a pretended riot at Fort Monckton on the Gosport side of the harbour. As the news spread, crowds ran to the Fort and when the Captain saw that he had obtained his object, he silently placed a party of marines at the end of Haslar Bridge, the only way out, and took every man who answered his purpose as he returned from the scene of the false alarm".

Another terror that alarmed the residents of Gosport came from the large number of French prisoners housed at Forton. About 4,000 of these poor wretches were crowded into the wooden and stone barracks and in several hulks moored in Forton Creek. There were also convicts charged with treason or with piracy. Two grim cemeteries situated near the present swimming bath at St. Vincent were crammed to overflowing, the ghastly conditions of the prisons meant that a third of the inmates died before release. The prisoners spent their time in wild gambling, often gambling away all their clothes and being forced to go naked, sometimes gambling away their food for months ahead, meagre as it was. Stories were told of wild and savage duels on the slightest pretext. Knives and forks were given out at each meal to prevent them becoming weapons in gambling duels but other more deadly weapons were improvised. There was a duel fought in 1813 when one man put too much salt in another's soup. The prisoners also spent time in making baskets and exquisitely carved ships in full rigging, from old bones. These they sold to the numerous visitors.

On the evening of the 22nd July, 1807 the bells of Forton prison rang out. The old wooden barracks was a mass of flames. At the time this building was being repaired and the fire was probably caused by the upsetting of a cauldron of boiling pitch which was being heated in the workshop. On this occasion the prisoners behaved admirably and helped to put the fire out.

Another threat to the citizens of Gosport came from the numerous attempts at escape by the prisoners. Sometimes they were successful, at other times the fugitives were caught and executed. In 1812 three prisoners on parole got away from Forton and made their way down to the harbour. There they hired a waterman named George Brothers, telling him they were sailors making their way back to their ship in Spithead. Once they got outside the harbour they offered him a bribe to help them but he refused and tried to signal his plight to nearby ships in Spithead. The fugitives stabbed him and threw his body overboard. The incident was seen from the shore and boats set out in pursuit. Eventually, however, the fugitives were overtaken and subsequently executed at Winchester.

All the romance and intrigue of the period is best shown in the astonishing career of the Reverend Richard Bingham who was vicar of Holy Trinity from 1807 (when he succeeded his father) until he died at the age of 93 in 1858. Isaac Moody Bingham, the father, became curate of Holy Trinity in 1779 and 11 years later, 1790, his son Richard came to help him. The father was incumbent until the 30th January 1807 when at the age of 73 he died, as the memorial tablet to him says "Beloved, honoured, and lamented by all who knew the Goodness and Integrity of His heart". He had twelve children, one of whom, Richard took Holy Orders and became his assistant.

About Richard, however, the wildest tales circulated particularly during the early years of the century. He was described at the time as the "notorious Richard Bingham, B.A., Fellow of New College, Minister of Gosport Chapel and curate of Maresfield". Bingham was frequently in scrapes with the local populace and the law. Two years before taking up duties in Gosport he had landed himself in matrimonial troubles. He married the eldest daughter of Sir Charles Douglas who had declared in his will that she should not receive anything from his estate if she married Richard or any other son of

John Moody Bingham. But father's name was not John, it was Isaac and Richard brought an action to have the will set aside. The House of Lords held that the intention of Sir Charles Douglas was perfectly clear despite the wrong rendering of Isaac as John and dismissed the claim.

Richard no sooner came to Gosport than he began to get into debt. The Binghams lived in a tall house called The Hall built at the end of the 18th century. The house was on the eastern side of the church very close to the mud flats of the harbour mouth at the secluded entrance to Haslar Creek. It was said that a cellar ran from the harbour to the house and thence by an underground passage into the church itself. The most fantastic stories of contraband running circulated through the town. It was declared that when his creditors arrived at The Hall, Bingham hid in the underground passage or slipped through into the church. On one occasion his irate, demanding, creditors turned up with a battering ram to break down his door, but Richard was supposed to have escaped through the underground route into the church. It was said he was in league with smugglers, that he knew when the Press gangs were about, and that his spies in the local pubs kept him informed of all the opportunities for an illegal deal. All this was denied in 1803 when a statement was issued about "the fallacy of the many reports which have been of late industriously circulated to his prejudice, after having for thirteen years performed the duties of his office with punctuality, zeal and ability". His detractors declared that he had written this testimonial himself.

Matters came to a head in 1810 when Bingham was tried on charges of writing threatening letters to his parishioners (many of whom were his creditors) and with arson of his own house. Bingham was acquitted on these counts. He himself took the view that because he was a magistrate as well as a parson and because the people of Gosport were especially vicious he was constantly ill-used. "The punctual performance of the duties of a Magistrate must always excite a host of foes and peculiarly so in a town of which the principal part of the population consists of such persons as those of whom it is composed in Gosport". He spoke of the "illwill, acrimony and dislike of the people of a place so constituted as Gosport".

A few years later, in 1813, Richard Bingham was again embroiled in a case of fraud and conspiracy at Winchester Assizes and on this occasion he was convicted and sent to prison for six months. The circumstances were typical of the time. Richard, as a Magistrate sitting at Fareham was responsible, with his colleagues, for granting licences for public houses. Richard himself owned the "Revolutionaire" in Beach Street which was leased to Nicholas Breach. The military authorities decided in 1803 to tear down several houses in Beach Street in order to improve the defences. The "Revolutionaire" was one of the places to go. Nicholas Breach was compensated and for some years was given a licence although he had no public house to attach it to. Bingham was alleged to have evolved the brilliant scheme of buying two houses for £700 and selling them (with the redundant licence) for £2,200, taking care to dodge some Stamp Duty by having £1,900 rather than £2,200 put in the conveyance. The buyer, one James Cooper, declared he had been defrauded because he had previously been offered the two houses at a cheaper price but had been warned off by Bingham.

There was a great deal of local scandal. James Cooper was already the tenant of the Dover Castle public house. He claimed that Bingham had employed an agent named Watts who was a "man of straw" in order to cover up a profit of £1,500 which would cancel a debt Bingham owed to Cooper. Cooper asserted that he had made heavy loans to Bingham. Bingham on his side declared the whole matter was a conspiracy engineered by two of his brother magistrates who were brewers and seeking revenge because Bingham had supported applications for licences against their interests. Cooper was a pawn in the game.

Anyhow, although the parish church and its surrounds fell into such decay that a special Act of Parliament had to be obtained in 1825, Bingham lived through all his troubles as vicar of Holy Trinity until the ripe old age of 93 and when he died on 18th July 1858 he was buried in the churchyard. His son, Richard Bingham the Younger, was his curate at Holy Trinity for 22 years, from 1822-44.

As we shall see he was most remembered in succeeding generations for the opening up of the housing area of Newtown, or as it was known for a long period Bingham Town, immediately beyond the ramparts of the old town on the roadway to Alverstoke.

One delightful incident which occurred on 7th August 1800 concerns the beating of the bounds of Portsmouth. As we have seen, under a Charter of Charles II's reign in 1682, Gosport was annexed to Portsmouth. Later, however, it was discovered that an earlier Charter of Charles I had never been surrendered and since it gave much more favourable terms to the city it was brought back into effective operation and remained the governing instrument of Portsmouth until the Municipal Corporations Act of 1835. Notwithstanding, Portsmouth claimed jurisdiction over the whole of the waters of the harbour extending up the creeks of Gosport and Fareham. The story is told in "The Annals of Portsmouth" by W. H. Saunders how on the 7th August 1800 according to ancient custom the Corporation of Portsmouth beat the bounds of the Borough. They left in several barges. The first had a band, the second the Mayor and Aldermen in their scarlet robes, the Town Clerk and the Sergeant-at-Mace bearing the Mace, over which was flying the Corporation flag of silk with the Borough crest in the centre. The procession left Sally Port and went first to the boundary post on Southsea beach, where the Mayor, Mr. Goldson, and Mr. James Carter performed the time honoured ceremony of flogging each other round the post to impress its situation on their memory. The boats then proceeded up the harbour and on reaching the Gosport shore the Sergeant-at-Mace touched the shore with an oar and the Town Clerk, on behalf of the Mayor, Aldermen and Burgesses, claimed jurisdiction "In as full and ample a manner as was ever claimed and enjoyed by any of the Mayors or his predecessors". This ceremony was repeated at several points along the shore but there was fighting in Haslar Creek and at Fareham. The people threatened to duck the Mayor and Aldermen in their robes if they dared to step on shore, so they departed.

CHAPTER 9

Gosport in the Early 19th Century

So far we have traced the story of Gosport during the centuries and have seen it emerge from a tiny hamlet of poor fishermen to an important naval town in 1800. The development came during the long period of war in the 18th century. After 1815 there was, in the main, a period of peace. That provides us with a clue and a warning. At the auction sale in 1791, referred to in an earlier chapter, Thomas Ayling sold a grocer's shop which was let to one John Burton Trimmings on a yearly lease of £30 in time of peace and £40 in time of war. War brought prosperity to local tradesmen. The bustle of a busy harbour, the fitting out of the fleet, the generosity of returning seamen, particularly in local pubs, with which the town abounded, all this brought increasing local wealth to the traders and the enterprising. Peace meant less activity.

But times could be hard for the poor, the widows, the aged and the families of men serving in the navy. Provisions could be scarce. During 1800 servants in Gosport were allowed only a quartern–loaf of bread a week and to alleviate the sufferings of the poor of Gosport and Portsmouth £900 was collected to buy Scotch herrings.

Rumour ran fast, of threatened invasion landings, of Press gang raids, of returning ships and those that had sunk with heavy loss of life. The mighty chain of iron, which was first stretched across the harbour mouth in 1522, had been renewed in 1664 by Edward Silvester who was paid £200 for the job, was felt by many local people to be the final safeguard for the harbour. During these years there were many demands that it be tightened as a defence precaution. The huge links were 3ft. 9in. in length and 3 inches thick, but it is unlikely that this would have saved the harbour.

Inside the harbour during the years before and after Trafalgar all was bustle. The ferrymen who knew the harbour waters and their currents reaped a rich harvest. There was constant crossing between Gosport, Portsmouth (the old town) and Portsea (the new dockyard area), not merely carrying passengers but stores and naval equipment. There was also a lucrative trade in carrying officers and ratings to their ships in the harbour or in Spithead. The ferrymen, rough, uncouth, but uncanny in their skill and knowledge of local waters, profited by the busy conditions war brought to Portsmouth Harbour. We have seen that during the period of Queen Elizabeth's reign the right to control the crossing of the ferry caused violent controversy. In 1800 it was the arrogance of the boat men, who demanded exorbitant amounts. Frequently the sailors who had come to Gosport for a gay time in love and pub and found themselves likely to be confronted with all the rigours of fierce naval discipline, preferred to pay the extravagant demands of the ferrymen rather than remain in Gosport.

By 1809 things had come to such a pass, complaints of abuses by the ferrymen had become so tumultous that a special Act of Parliament was obtained in an endeavour to curb the watermen and protect passengers.

The Act, which received Royal Assent on the 20th June 1809 was entitled "An Act for the better government of the Watermen working on the Passage between Gosport, Portsmouth and Portsea and other Places within Portsmouth Harbour, and to and from Spithead, St. Helens, and other Parts within the Isle of Wight in the County of Southampton . . . and for regulating the fares and such Watermen".

The preamble to the Act sets out the cause of the complaints. "Whereas the conduct of the watermen working on the passage between Gosport, in the parish of Alverstoke and Portsmouth and Portsea (and a number of other places are cited) by reason of their demanding exorbitant and unequal prices for the carriage of passengers and their refusing to carry passengers across the Harbour of Portsmouth and to and from Hardway, Fareham etc. . . . has long been complained of and is now become a general grievance and is a great inconvenience and detriment to the inhabitants of the said town and neighourhood, and also to the officers and seamen belonging to the said ships and vessels: may it please Your Majesty"—and here follows a list of local worthies from Gosport and Portsmouth, about 50 of them, who were to form a Commission for putting into execution "the several powers and authorities in and by this Act given". The list included the J.P.'s for the County of Southampton, the Mayor, Recorder and Aldermen of Portsmouth, the Steward of the Bishopric of Winchester for the time being, the Bishop's Bailiff of the Borough and Manor of Gosport for the time being and the Rector of Alverstoke. It also includes John Lind, Doctor of Physic (of Haslar) and William Burney, Doctor of Laws, head of the famous local academy in Clarence Square, for the education of naval officers.

The Commissioners—or any 7 of them—were to meet on the first Tuesday in the months of July, November and March annually, alternately in Gosport and Portsmouth. The first meeting was to be held at the India Arms, Gosport, on the first Tuesday in July following the passing of the Act. Only the relatively wealthy could be Commissioners—there was a property qualification (real estate £100, or personal property £2,500) and Commissioners had to be residents of the parish of Alverstoke or of Portsea or Portsmouth. Vacancies were filled in such a way as to give equal numbers on each side of the harbour.

Wide powers to fix the fares and regulate conditions were given to the Commissioners. There were to be two rates of fares—one to apply to crossing during the day time and in good weather, the other for crossing at night and in foul weather. And so that it should be beyond dispute, a blue flag was to be hoisted on the beach at Gosport to denote that foul weather fares were in operation. During fair weather the maximum number of passengers to a boat was ten—during foul weather it was six. The Commissioners could enforce the fares, they could fine any who demanded higher rates or refused to take passengers. A waterman who assaulted or insulted a passenger could be fined. The Commissioners could also examine and licence watermen and they were required to keep a book as a register of watermen. They could see that boats were kept in "good repair, order and condition and well and sufficiently provided with masts, sails, oars, rudder and all other proper gear and tackle".

Despite the meetings of the Commissioners at the India Arms in High Street, Gosport, the Act doesn't seem to have been very effective. The system of flags didn't work well, the watermen could not be expected to cross the harbour in really rough weather and they themselves were the best judges of weather conditions. On 5th May 1812 a second Act was passed. The preamble shows how inadequate was Parliament, faced with the Gosport watermen. "And whereas the said Act (of 1809) had been found ineffectual for answering the good purposes thereby intended, it is expedient that the same should be altered and amended". A new body of Commissioners was appointed—this time much more strongly representing the Navy— the Port Admiral of Portsmouth, the Junior Port Admiral, the Lieutenant Governor of Portsmouth—to join the previous Commissioners. The idea of having two rates of fares, one for fine and one for foul weather, was abandoned and the Commissioners were given much wider freedom to settle rates. The idea of flags being hoisted to denote dangerous weather or fine weather was retained. Three examiners were to be appointed to examine the watermen and to prepare the tables of rates and fares. Watermen were required to have spent three years as apprentices before being issued with a licence. The maximum number of passengers for a boat was still to be six in dangerous weather, but was limited to eight in fine weather. Meetings of the Commissioners were still to be held alternately at Gosport and Portsmouth.

Two features of the Act of 1812 are of particular interest. The Act laid considerable emphasis on the training of apprentices who were to become watermen—a three year period of apprenticeship had to be served before one could be licenced as a waterman. The Commissioners had wide powers to refuse to renew a licence. The other feature was that "for the encouragement of the watermen working on the said passage . . . it may be lawful for the said Commissioners to form and establish a fund for the purpose of relieving any decayed watermen working or who shall have been accustomed to work on the said passage, or of relieving the widows or children of any deceased watermen". Provision for training, for pensions and gratuities are far in advance of the general legislation of this period.

While this Act was reasonably effective in controlling the number of watermen and regulating the fares they could demand, the great profit of the trade came to an end with the end of the Napoleonic Wars in 1815. Life resumed a more steady pace once the great naval chiefs departed. Crossing the harbour became a more leisurely occupation.

Not all ferrymen were black sheep. In 1828 James Straycock of Great Yarmouth, in Norfolk, left the sum of £78 11s. 0d. new 4% annuities, "the dividends thereon were to be divided annually between two of the oldest and most respectable watermen residing in the parish of Alverstoke, to be selected by the Rector or Churchwardens; the object of such bequest being to manifest the donor's sense of an Act of Benevolence rendered him in being gratuitously ferried from Gosport to Portsmouth when he was sick and poor, and as an incentive to that class of man to do good when it is in their power".

Not again until the establishment of the floating bridge in 1840 did the problem of crossing the harbour to get to Portsmouth become serious. And then the issue was not so much pedestrian as vehicular traffic. It was solved in the year 1840 but a hundred years later was worse than ever.

In comparison with the rapid growth of the great northern and midland towns under the impetus of the Industrial Revolution, Gosport developed relatively slowly in the early 19th century. The population at the first successful census taken in 1821 was 10,342. Twenty years later in 1841 it was 13,510. But the vast majority still lived in huddled conditions within the ramparts. The most extensive development beyond the rampart and its moats was Bingham Town where rows of streets named after the sons (Joseph, Henry, etc.) of the parson and ale-house keeper, Richard Bingham, began to be erected.

The sanitary conditions within the town were quite shocking. There was no main drainage—cess pits or at best the town moat provided for the filth of the town, there was no piped water supply, the town abounded with wells—private wells of individual houses and town wells for general supply. The Act of 1763 "An Act for the better paving of the streets and for preventing nuisances and other annoyances in the town of Gosport in the County of Southampton", by which a body of Commissioners had been appointed had fallen into abeyance. In 1814 the situation had become so bad that a further Act was passed. The title of the Act is significant. "An Act for watching, lighting, and cleansing the town of Gosport in the County of Southampton and for amending and rendering more effectual an act passed in the third year of His present Majesty (1763) for better paving the streets and preventing nuisances and annoyances in the said town".

The Act of 1814 was obtained at a cost of £613 raised by local gentry, business men and shopkeepers. It established a body of 33 local magnates with wide powers to improve sanitary and general conditions within the town. The Commissioners were authorised to borrow £2,500 on the security of the rates they were empowered to levy. They set to work with the will of their predecessors but they soon found themselves confronted with serious difficulties. They had no jurisdiction outside the ramparts or over the area below high water mark. Nor was there much local enthusiasm. A few years later the local inhabitants rejected a proposal to adopt the first Public Health Act by 1007 votes to 626.

Whilst under the stress of war conditions Gosport had developed apace, it still remained for essential local government services part of the parish of Alverstoke, which was more than two miles distant. Rural life went on its way in Alverstoke although already some retired naval officers were taking up residence in the village near to Spithead and the Solent. The churchyard tells of their memorials. Such records as we have, and they are scanty, tell of a quiet undisturbed village clustered around its ancient church. In 1711 there is given in the Vestry Book a record of the communion plate and other belongings of the church. "One large silver flagon with Captain Player's coat of arms engrossed on it; one chalice and cover the gift of John Eames to the church; two silver plates with a cypher engraved on the back; one old fashioned silver bowl; one tin box with charters of this parish therein and the manumission of freedom". It is this tin box which is so intriguing for there is no mention of it after 1800 and its priceless records seem to have vanished with the box.

But the church warden's accounts tell a rural story:-

		£	s.	d.
1757	paid for a badger	0	1	0
1761	April 20 paid James Churcher for 3 foxes heads		3	0
1764	To Wm. Robinson for 5 foxes heads	0	5	0

1765	paid John Seagon for a wheel and hanging the new bell	2	15	0
1790	Expenses for treading the bounds of this parish	8	8	11
1791	Paid different persons for 150 dozen sparrows heads	1	1	8
1815	To Joshua Hunt for new stocks	1	12	0
1821	To 27 stoats and hedgehogs		9	0

This is a very different picture from the congested life of Gosport itself. Although parochial affairs might be run by the overseers, the church wardens, the Easter Vestry, the unpaid annually serving surveyor of highways of Alverstoke, changes were taking place in Gosport. After the dismantling of the old wooden market house in the High Street, numerous proposals were made for a new assembly hall more in keeping with the growing size and importance of the town. One scheme, seriously considered, was of a lottery with prizes of £25 each. In the end a special Act of Parliament was secured in 1811, with the consent of the Bishop of Winchester, for the erection of a new market house almost on the shore of the harbour near to the site of the ancient fair. A large square colonnaded building of white stone was finally erected. Below there was a bonding house and above a court house. The Act of 1811 was amended by a further Act passed 1828 which gave the Trustees of the Market House very wide powers embracing not only the market house itself but the two annual fairs held nearby on May 4th and October 10th. By these Acts the Trustees had special powers over two pieces of waste land, on one of which the Market House was erected and on the other the fairs were held. Right to control the fairs included powers to levy tolls "upon such things as are normally sold at fairs and of collecting rents for stalls". These rights gave rise to a great deal of local controversy later on in the century.

The men of Gosport were intensely patriotic as well as conscious of the important part they had played in the years of war. When George III came to Portsmouth in 1773 he crossed the harbour to inspect the new brewery at Weovil. His popularity was increased by a grant of £2,100 to be distributed among the workers in the Dockyard; the poor of Portsmouth, Portsea and Gosport receiving £250. But it was in 1813, toward the end of the long struggle with France, that the monarch came again. The story is told that he intended to proceed to Brighton the next day but "on hearing that the loyal inhabitants of the ancient Borough of Gosport had resolved to address him, he altered his arrangements and received on board his yacht at Spithead a deputation consisting of The Mayor, General Neville, Rev. Charles Augustus North, S. Jellicoe, William Burney, LL.D., William Page, Robert Curry, Captain Carter and Captain Halstead". There was abundant evidence of loyalty—but there wasn't a Mayor of Gosport nor was it an ancient Borough.

Perhaps that is as well. Gosport although much larger than many of the Boroughs of Hampshire was not an incorporated town. In consequence a vigorous religious life developed which in incorporated towns was impossible under the religious laws of the time. The dissenters had founded a flourishing chapel in the town well before 1700, possibly as early as 1663. The first Minister, Rev. William Marshall, ministered to his flock in the early 18th century. By 1794 a new enlarged church of considerable proportions was erected in the High Street. It was largely the results of the efforts of a remarkable man, Rev. David Bogue, who became minister to the Gosport independent chapel in 1774. He lived in Gosport until his death in 1825. He was one of the founders of what became the London Missionary Society and established in High Street, Gosport, an academy for the training of missionaries. One of his students was David Livingstone. Since the town was not an incorporated borough the Roman Catholics were enabled to establish a successful church.

While the churches of the Dissenters and of the Catholics were flourishing, matters were very different at Holy Trinity where the notorious Bingham was in charge. The church was so badly neglected that in 1825 an Act of Parliament was obtained for the "perpetual maintenance and support of the Chapel of the Holy and Undivided Trinity in the town of Gosport". The Act, which obtained Royal Assent on 20th May 1825, sets out the details of the erection and enlargement of the church and then goes on to say that there is no legal method of making and levying rates for the repairs to the church and that the walls have fallen into decay. It enables the Churchwardens to levy a rate of 1/- in the £ upon the proprietors of pews or seats. Another clause is very significant. "If any person or persons shall wilfully or maliciously injure, pull down or break any tree or window, stones or monuments, or during the time of divine service shall play at Football or any other game of sport or discharge firearms or fireworks in the said yard or street adjoining thereto or make any noise to the disturbance of the congregation assembled in the said Chapel . . . for every such offence he should forfeit and pay a sum not exceeding 40/- and not less that 5/-".

In 1828 it was decided by the Admiralty to transfer the whole of the Victualling Department of the navy from Portsea to Clarence Yard. This was in part due to the more commodious premises available but also largely in consequence of the scandals that had arisen from the constant thieving in the storage yards. A contemporary writer gives this account of the Royal Clarence Yard. "The arrangements which are all upon the most extensive scale are disposed in such capital order that not the slightest difficulty ever arises in supplying any number of ships with provisions at a moment's notice. The first set of store-houses contains rum, tea, wine, tobacco, and cocoa. Next follows the beer store and the brewery in which is prepared and kept the beer for the Royal Naval hospitals and Marine Infirmaries, then comes the cooperage. Next we have six meat stores each of which is capable of holding 9,000 tons of salt provisions, then comes one large and three small provision stores and after these stores, which contain among other things Bibles, tracts and the Life of Nelson, comes the bread store".

CHAPTER 10

Gosport during the period 1830-40

One of the most exciting days in Gosport was the 1st August 1832. It was a Tuesday, marvellously sunny and gay. The occasion was the celebration of the 1832 Reform Bill which after many controversies had been passed by Parliament. Across the High Street banners fluttered in the warm breeze with their slogans "Magna Charter of 1832, King, Lords and Commons". More to the point all the shops were closed and a great feast of roast beef and plum pudding was prepared.

At 2.30 p.m. the procession through the town moved off, the leaders carrying the silken banners. One read "We are a patient but a determined people" while another was inscribed Earl Grey and Reform". From the India Arms to North Cross Street, tables were laid. From Clarence Square where the procession had assembled, round to the High Street flags were flown. The band played "God save the King" and "The Roast Beef of Old England", the Reverend Mr. Veck said grace and the company sat down to celebrate. There were barrels of beer, pounds of tobacco. There followed a wild hilarious night of feasting, drinking, bonfires, dancing and cheers to usher in the new age of democratic government.

But the claim for democracy demands the provision of education— what is the use of giving the citizen the vote (indeed most of those who joined in the celebration did not achieve the vote) unless he can read and understand the papers? So, in 1831 the first school was opened. The site which was on the west side of Holy Trinity Church, was bought for £300 and it was intended that the premises, described as a "commodious building" would be erected for less than that sum so that the whole school would cost less than £600. Another school was commenced at Forton St. John's shortly afterwards and was reputed to have the honour of being the one school in Gosport visited by Queen Victoria.

The enthusiasm for education grew during the 1840-50 period. The National School at Alverstoke was established in 1842, the St. Matthew's School attached to the new parish, was erected in 1844-45 and a further new school, this time at Elson, was built in 1849. Until then practically the only education available was in private schools. The famous Burney's Academy at Coldharbour was established during the late 1780's and won a world wide reputation for the standard of its education in seamanship. The papers advertised the school in 1800. "At the Academy, delightfully situated in Cold Harbour Gosport, a limited number of young gentlemen are genteely boarded, tenderly treated, and instructed in every branch of useful and polite literature by William Burney A.M. Math. The school has long been established and the plan upon which it is conducted is liberal and extensive and particularly calculated for youth intended for the Navy and Army". The school was very much of a forcing academy; Burney who wrote, or at least edited, a Marine Dictionary ruled the school for about 40 years. But from early days it received royal patronage. King William IV gave it a 14 oared boat known as the King's Cutter and a succcession of royal princes were enrolled as pupils. The Burney family controlled the Academy—it was even allowed to call itself The Royal Academy—for about 100 years. There was a boarding school for boys at Stoke Cottage and several boarding schools for girls as well as a number of privately owned day schools.

The St. Matthew's School was built before the new church from which it got its name. In those days £1,000 was a handsome sum with which to build a school and the St. Matthew's, considered the finest school in the town, cost at least £1,100. The new church looked out on the ramparts and the archways which led out of the town. One archway was for incoming traffic, the second for outgoing traffic and the third, a much smaller one, was for pedestrians only. The arches and the gates remained until 1883. The new parish of St. Matthew covered a considerable part of the northern side of the town. It was bounded by the ramparts, the creeks and the High Street. It included some of the most congested parts of the district—Blackbear Yard, Brandy Mount, Griffiths Rents and Dark Alley—names reminiscent of the back alleyways of a highly romantic sea town.

A further indication of the new age of progress came in 1834. Until then the town had relied upon old oil lamps for private houses and at the corner of some streets. They gave a flicker of light. But now a new gas company was formed and a gas-works erected in the growing area just outside the town. The new system of lighting was the subject of considerable controversy and bitter opposition, since many believed the gas pipes would explode and wreck their homes. But finally gas lamps replaced oil lamps in the streets and alleys.

A little later came the provision of a piped water supply. Away back in 1698 an enterprising Londoner named Thomas Lewis had attempted to establish a piped supply and had obtained an Act of Parliament for the erection of a waterworks at Forton but the Company got into financial troubles and only about 240 houses were ever supplied with water through the hollowed out elm-tree pipes that were then used. The normal method of supplying water in the 1830-1840 period was by water carts which drew their supplies from the large number of wells in the district and which sold water by the bucket at a ¼d. a bucketful. Even in 1850 there were 36 water carts, each capable of carrying a ton of water, and although its quality was not too good and its supply intermittent the water vendors collected over £1,700 a year. But the new water Company was not established until 1858.

But by far the most significant sign of the changing times was the opening of the railway line between Gosport and London. In 1841 the London and South Western Railway Company decided to purchase property in Spring Garden Lane belonging to Mr. Isaac Legg. The garden was turned into an elaborate station with rows of columns on either side. It was designed by the distinguished and fashionable architect, Sir William Tite. Adjacent was a spacious hotel—the Station Tavern Hotel. It was on the 7th February 1842 that the new station was officially opened and a passenger train service, which lasted for about 100 years, commenced. Fast trains to London capable of 20 miles an hour were advertised. The single fare on the fast train was 22/-. But you could also travel by the slow stopping train in an open wagon for 8/6. The coming of the railway made a tremendous difference especially as there was no direct railway communication between London and Portsmouth until June 1847. Previous to this stage-coaches provided the only link with distant parts. Coaches ran from Mr. Padwick's office at the bottom of the High Street (then Middle Street). The Telegraph started for London at 5 a.m. and returned the following day. The Yeoman left the India Arms for Piccadilly each morning at 8.45. Other coaches left the India Arms for Salisbury and the west country.

The coming of the railway made the traffic across the harbour more important. It also provided a direct route between Gosport and the Isle of Wight. A ferry to take horses and light carriages across the harbour had been built in 1834. In 1838 a new Company was formed with the object of building a floating bridge which would take quite heavy vehicles across the harbour, in order to avoid the long trek round for vehicles through Fareham, Portchester and finally to Portsmouth, a journey that was known locally as "Going round the Victory". By May 1840 the floating bridge was ready for use. Its first crossing of the harbour on 11th May 1840, was a matter for universal local rejoicing. Combined with the new railway it provided the quickest, safest and cheapest way of sending goods from Portsmouth to London. The link to the Isle of Wight came in 1842 when a pier was built at Stokes Bay and the Gosport railway line connected to it.

The new line to the Isle of Wight opened in April 1863 when a branch line to Stokes Bay was established linking with the new pier. The journey to Ryde was made by the shortest route possible and for a time was very popular. Passengers from London and still more from the Midlands were able to join the ferry steamer direct from the train. In Portsmouth the old station at the Landport was, until 1876, the nearest one could get to the pier for the island. But it took nearly as long to get the Gosport-Stokes Bay Railway established as it lasted as a practical proposition. A private Act of Parliament authorising the promotion of the scheme was passed in August, 1855, but the line wasn't commenced until 1859 nor finally opened until April, 1863, when the old London and South Western Railway took over its operation. The ferry boat to Ryde was an old paddle boat—the Garelock. A loop line was constructed in 1865 to avoid the necessity for going into the Gosport terminus and through coaches conveyed passengers from London, via Basingstoke, Eastleigh, Fareham direct to Stokes Bay pier. The journey took about 2½ hours. In 1915 during the first world war the route ceased to be used and in 1922 the pier became the property of the Admiralty.

In the 1840 period great changes were occurring in the life of the navy and they changed the pattern of life for Gosport. Queen Victoria, who ascended the throne in 1837, held the first Naval Review in 1842 and for the rest of the century Naval Reviews were matters of great social importance. In 1845 came the last Review at Spithead of the old sailing warships. The old wooden bulwarks were giving place to iron and the great canvas sails to steam. At Spithead during this year two ships were set against eah other. One was the paddle steamer "The Alecto", the other "The Ratler" with a screw propeller. Both were of the same tonnage and power and had identical equipment. They were fastened securely stern to stern, the engines set and then at a given signal full steam ahead was ordered. "The Ratler" won easily, towing "The Alecto" at two and a half knots despite the frantic and furious churning of the paddles. The day of the ironclad had arrived and the use of the screw propeller was settled.

But in the town more interest was shown in a celebrated trial of another kind. On Southsea Beach stood the Kings's Rooms, a fashionable meeting place for members of the services. Captain Seton of the 11th Dragoons there met the wife of Lieutenant C. Hawkey of the Royal Marines and paid her lavish but allegedly, unwelcome attentions. Hawkey called Seton to account after a dance and threatened him with the alternatives of a public horsewhipping in Portsmouth High Street or a duel with pistols. The two met at Browndown between Alverstoke and Lee-on-the-Solent and as a result Seton was mortally wounded. Hawkey was charged at

Winchester Assizes with the manslaughter of Seton but was acquitted on the grounds that he had been provoked by Seton's dastardly conduct and the death of Captain Seton had really been due to the result of an operation performed by the surgeons to extract the bullet. But so great was the public scandal and so sensational the newspaper accounts of the incident that it was the last formal duel of its kind.

For some years Gosport had been increasing in importance. In 1828 the entire Victualling Department was established at Clarence Yard. This was partly owing to the greater space available upon which more satisfactory premises could be erected and partly to the unfortunate reputation which the department at King Street in Portsmouth had acquired.

The population of the town was increasing, although rather slowly. At the Census of 1821 it was recorded at 10,342—a quite sizeable town for the period. By 1841 it had reached 13,510. But still it was very much of a walled town with little expansion outside the moats and walls. A publication of 1837 desribes the variety of rural rides and walks from Alverstoke, one of them through "a large hamlet called Bingham Town, to the Town of Gosport".

Local government during this period presented a confused and bewildering pattern. Gosport town was still under the direction or dominance of the parish of Alverstoke. The Acts setting up bodies of commissioners for special purposes did not prove satisfactory. In 1834 under the new Poor Law Act a Board of Guardians was established. Under the much older Gilberts Act a local workhouse had been built and equipped in South Street but the newly elected Board of Guardians set to work to erect between Gosport and Alverstoke, close by the Alver Creek, a large, spacious, but grim workhouse. When the Municipal Corporations Act was passed in 1835 Gosport was not included as one of the new towns to receive a municipal charter. In fact there was no effective local government until 1851, when after years of quite serious outbreaks of cholera and typhoid the 1848 Public Health Act was adopted and a local Board of Health began to function. The method of voting for this body was particularly interesting. Ballot papers were taken round to the houses of those people who were on the electoral roll. Later they were called for by the parish officers. Everybody got a ballot form but this method of collecting votes obviously led to a considerable amount of abuse.

CHAPTER 11

Gosport 1850-1860

In an earlier chapter we looked at Gosport in the 1750–60 period when the town was becoming fortified with ramparts and a moat and the tempo of life within was being affected by the long French wars. A hundred years later, in 1850–60 the threat of war was to lead to a new line of fortifications further out from the harbour town centre, and which set a new limit to its urban development.

For our survey of Gosport in the middle of the 19th century we can look at the first Ordnance Survey map and the Post Office guide. Gosport town itself within the area of the ramparts was then as thickly peopled with tenements, rents and alleyways as any town in the country. The population was growing fairly quickly. As we have seen, in 1821 the parish of Alverstoke (which included Gosport) had 10,341 inhabitants and by 1841 it had grown to 13,587. At the next census, in 1851, it was 16,908 and by 1861 it had reached 22,653. Of the 16,908 in the parish in 1851, no less than 9,846 lived in the Liberty of Gosport, that is within the congested area of the town. In 1851 there were 104 courtyards and alleyways and in them some 750 densely populated tenement houses. Some of these, built spaciously in the 18th century for sea captains, were now becoming derelict hovels in which every room housed at least one family under pestilential conditions.

But to the outside visitor Gosport presented an attractive, if quaint, appearance. The Kelly's Post Office Directory for 1855 describes it thus, "Gosport is a sea port and market and railway town, and although not incorporated, it is styled, in congratulatory addresses to the Crown, as 'the ancient town and borough of Gosport'. Its local government, so far as respects the paving and lighting of the town, consists of a body of trustees, appointed under certain Acts of Parliament, the principle of which is self-election, the inhabitants and ratepayers having no voice or control in the appointment of the functionaries by whom they are taxed". In fact the 33 trustees went on as the main form of local government, outside the parish officers and the Board of Guardians, until after 1870.

The Directory continues "Gosport occupies a small peninsula (and has risen to importance as a convenient appendage to Portsmouth) on the opposite side of the harbour, projecting into its mouth to within half a mile of Portsmouth, and the transit to and fro is actively maintained by means of a ferry: in addition to which a floating bridge was constructed about 1837 for the conveyance of passengers, coaches, wagons, cattle etc. and which adds much to the convenience and to the intercourse of the towns of Gosport and Portsmouth. In the year 1843 a floating pier was opened for the accommodation of the public, ladies and children can embark and disembark at all times of tide, it being so constructed as to be always on a level with the deck of the steamers".

Describing the town itself the Directory says "Gosport is a well-built, handsome town but appears to most advantage in the approach by water, as its finest buildings line the coast. Beside this it has a principal street, extending westward from the ferry, other parallel streets and several intersecting them. About a quarter of a mile from the town is the Gosport terminus of the London and South Western Railway from which there is an additional extension for the convenience of Her Majesty (Queen Victoria) for embarking and disembarking on board her yacht at the Royal Clarence Yard".

Of the trading life of the town the accounts says "There are several breweries, shipyards and a considerable trade chiefly in articles for the supply of the army and navy. The markets held on Tuesday, Thursday and Saturday are abundantly furnished with fish and vegetables and very well frequented. The fairs are held on the 4th May and the 10th October". Later in the century the fair came into disrepute and was the subject of a great deal of local agitation.

The statement claimed that "the land side is fortified from Weovill to the shores of Alverstoke Lake by strong lines, bastions, redoubts and counterscarps" although, as we shall see, the experts had quite different views as to the practical usefulness of these fortifications.

On the north side of Gosport the account tells of "the Royal Clarence victualling yard where are the brewery, cooperage, biscuit-baking department and an immense range of storehouses connected with those departments of the service. About a mile north is Forton Lake, a large basin, or creek of the harbour, which admits vessels of considerable burthen. On Priddy's Hard, north of the lake, and connected with the harbour by a small cut through the sands, is the strongly arched bombproof magazine for powder. Near it are the ruins of Borough Castle, traditionally ascribed to King Stephen, and now used as a burial ground for convicts".

On the southern side of Gosport—"about a mile south, on the other side of Alverstoke Lake, is Haslar Hospital for sick and wounded marines". The account goes on to describe the grandeur of Haslar and proceeds "Three quarters of a mile south west from the hospital is Monckton Fort, a regular and very strong fortification, from which 42

84

pieces of heavy ordnance may be brought to bear on an opposing force".

Alverstoke at this period was very much the residential area, a picturesque village grouped around its ancient church, and yet the parochial centre of a wide area which extended to Anglesey, Elson, Forton and Hardway. The account records the establishment in 1842 of "a national school of large dimensions" of which at this time Henry Hill was the master. An omnibus ran daily at noon the two miles to Gosport and to the South-Western terminus station.

Near to Alverstoke—a little nearer to the shore—was Anglesey or Angleseyville. "This beautiful village of modern date and commanding extensive views of the Isle of Wight, Spithead, and the Motherbank, the first stone having been laid by the Marquis of Anglesey in the year 1826. A chapel of ease was opened in 1844, dedicated to St. Mark. Here is a large hotel, reading rooms, baths and public gardens. The situation is very elevated and the surrounding scenery so commands universal admiration for its beauty and great variety, and in summer months, it is much frequented by gentry for the benefit of its sea bathing and the beauties of its scenery". No traders lived at Anglesey, only gentry—and these resided in The Crescent or in St. Mark's Place.

Out from Gosport, about a mile from Gosport Station on the old road from Gosport to Southampton, was the growing area of Forton, with, in 1851, some 3,260 inhabitants. A feature of the area was the handsome new church, built about 1830 and dedicated to St. John the Evangelist. The national school where Mr. Charles J. Maynard ruled as master was of recent construction. A large military prison with an imposing facade and entry porch but with 150 grim cells stood nearby. The most important feature of Forton, however, was the Forton Barracks which had by this time become the home of the Royal Marines. By 1820 the four main blocks of the new establishments were built. Originally they were intended to provide a new military hospital but until 1848 they were in the possession of the Ordnance Department. On 29th March, 1848, the Marines (Royal Marine Light Infantry) known as the Reds took over the buildings. The story goes that the Marines, previously at Hilsea, were transferred to Forton because the Lieutenant-Governor found that he could not command their services for army displays in the area. Be that as it may the Reds remained in occupation until 1923 when they were amalgamated with the Blues and returned to Hilsea. Forton Barracks stood empty for four years.

During their occupancy the Marines greatly extended and developed Forton Barracks. New areas were acquired between 1848 and 1856, part of the foreshore of the creek was reclaimed to provide a swimming bath. In 1858 the old Millpond was purchased from the Bishop of Winchester and reclaimed to provide a sportsfield. Much of the development of the barracks was, in 1850-60, still in the future, but Colonel James Irvin Willes, the Commandant of the Royal Marines was at this time a person of great importance in the life of Gosport.

By contrast with Forton, Brockhurst was at this time a small village with a dozen or so gentry living there and about a dozen small traders. Cottages were clustered on each side of the main roadway from Gosport. Perhaps the most important resident was the formidable headmaster and proprietor of the famous academy at Coldharbour, Dr. the Honourable Charles Burney, LL.D., of Brockhurst Lodge.

Even smaller was the scattered district of Elson and Hardway with its population of 1,059 in 1851. A new church, described as a "neat stone building" was erected in 1845, the cost being met partly by subscription and partly by government grant and just beyond the village a stone constructed "national" school was established about the same time.

For the rest of what is now comprised in the Borough of Gosport, only the parish of Rowner is significant. Rowner was at that time in the Hundred of Titchfield and for poor law purposes in the Union of Fareham. Although it comprised 1,191 acres there were in 1851 only 133 inhabitants in the small village around the ancient church. The Grange was a notable farmhouse.

Once outside the comparative bustle of the town of Gosport and the village centre of Alverstoke, there were large areas of rough ground with little communication between the hamlets and certainly no sense of belonging to a built up area. From Brockhurst Cross to Elson there was neither a road nor a house. Two names shown on the contemporary map of the Hardway area are symbolic of the time and the area—Hurricane House and Jack in the Bush—but they have both disappeared. Beyond that, Frater Lake is marked, Bedenham appears as a single house, while Foxbury Point and Fleetlands Park are shown. Bridgemary is no more than a small farm. From Brown Down on the Solent coast to Chark Common and Rowner is indicated as an extensive area of marshland.

Within the town itself in the 1850's there was considerable activity. From the India Arms in the High Street, Hyslop's horse omnibus went to the station to meet every train. The Old Northumberland, conveniently sited near the Ferry, was a main posting house. Carriers' vans and public coaches were still in demand. Boyce ran a service to Southampton from the Old Northumberland, Gosport, to the Nag's Head, Salisbury, on Tuesdays, Thursdays and Saturdays at 3 p.m. while his rival Stubbs did the same service on Mondays, Wednesdays and Fridays at 3 p.m. Boyce also had a service to Titchfield three times a week while Sait ran one to Fareham twice a week. From the Floating Pier in the Harbour there was a ferry to Ryde daily.

The High Street of Gosport was already becoming a busy commercial centre. There were two main banks, the Portsmouth, Portsea, Gosport and South Hants Banking Company (Gosport Branch), 41 High Street, whose Manager was John Charles Devereux and the Bank of Deposit and National Assurance and Investment Society with a branch at 58 High Street. Nearly all the insurance companies, many of which have passed out of existence as separate entities, had their agents in Gosport. Of the 29 recorded, 13 were established in the High Street and most of the others in North Street. Many of the public offices were in the High Street too. Many people who were destined to play an important part in the life of Gosport later in the century were established in office by this time. There was William Fitchett Burrel of 25 Coldharbour who was clerk and solicitor to the Gosport and Haslar Bridge Company and also Clerk to the Proprietors of the Gosport Market Place. There was David Compigne the local Director of the South Hants Banking Company, Clerk to the Commissioners of Paving and Secretary of the Gosport Gas Company and Thomas Henry Field the Actuary to the Gosport Savings Bank. There was Emery Churcher of the Stamp Office in the High Street.

Churches within Gosport in 1855 were numerous. There was the Holy Trinity Church where Richard Bingham, now almost 90 years old, was still incumbent, the new St. Matthew's erected on the Barrack field near the barracks, there was the famous Catholic Church in the High Street where Father Angelo Baldaconni ministered to a large flock, there were the Independent and the New Independent Churches in the High Street, a Primitive Methodist in North Street and a Wesleyan in the High Street. As to schools within Gosport, the Roman Catholics had a school behind their church where Mr. William Lyons and his daughter, Miss Fanny Lyons, were master and mistress. There was a British (nonconformist) school in the High Street, attached to the Independent Church. There was the Gosport free (girls) school in North Street where Mrs. James Johns Guyatt had in her charge a number of the poorer children. Of the National Schools, the most important was the Trinity School in Haslar Street, where George Snook was headmaster. The newest and most architecturally attractive school was St. Matthew's at Barrack Field.

Immediately outside the church were the ramparts and the moat which were supposed to fortify the town. At three points, there were arches and gates, one near the St. Matthew's Church controlling the Forton road out to Fareham and Southampton, one controlling the High Street out to Bingham Town, Stoke, Bury and Alverstoke and the third to the south guarding the road to Haslar. Three arches stretched across the road out to Forton. Two were for vehicles entering and leaving the town, and one, a much smaller one, was for pedestrians. They remained a feature of the town until they were taken down in 1883. A special cutting through the ramparts and across the moat had to be made to take the extension of the railway line from Gosport Station to the pier in Royal Clarence Yard. The arches were guarded daily by the military. For the inhabitants of Gosport the most popular Sunday afternoon walk was along the top of the ramparts. As a pleasant walk the ramparts were attractive but as a defence against invasion they were described in 1853 as "little better than field works consisting of an earthen rampart, without outworks"—the only defence against attack being a shallow moat of very miserable dimensions. It was estimated by the experts that Gosport could not withstand an attack for more than ten days. It was in these circumstances that the government, alarmed at the defenceless position of Gosport, determined to undertake a major construction of a defensive line of forts and moats some three miles west and north of Gosport, partly to defend Gosport itself but mainly to protect Portsmouth and its harbour from a French landing on the Solent coast.

Within the town, confined as it was, congestion was appalling and disease rampant. Only a few years before, in 1812, Gosport had been described as "The lovely sister of the matchless three"—Portsmouth, Portsea and Gosport—"the country around it is pleasant, with a mild air, abounding in fine gardens and delightful walks. The neighbourhood is considered far more healthy than Portsmouth being favoured with more land air and situated upon higher ground". But this description could not apply to the crowded insanitary conditions within the town and when in 1847 cholera affected the Portsmouth district, Gosport suffered seriously. It is understandable for the 33 commissioners had little powers and less knowledge of how to combat an outbreak of infectious diseases. All the water had to be carted in great water carts, except where householders had their own wells, while great sewage tuns carried out the garbage. Back-to-back courtyards, with open cess pits, narrow dark alleyways and crowded tenements were the main feature of the life of the poorer people. But there was one district that was the fashionable residential centre—particularly for naval officers—Coldharbour—or Clarence Square as it was now called with its wonderfully built 18th century houses and its famous school, Burney's Academy, where royalty was under instruction.

CHAPTER 12

The Fortification of Gosport

During the 1850-60 period there was constant rivalry between England and France and the danger of open warfare with a French invasion was constantly in the minds of English service chiefs. The aggressive diplomacy of Lord Palmerston, the rise to power of Napoleon III and the frequent clashes of policy between the two countries led people to quote the famous words of the Duke of Wellington: "I am bordering on seventy-seven years passed in honour. I hope that the Almighty may protect me from being a witness of the tragedy I cannot persuade my contemporaries to take measures to avert". The tragedy he contemplated was a full scaled French invasion of the south coast.

It was always realised the gravest danger would arise from a capture of Portsmouth and a consequent crippling of the British navy. And in this situation the key to the position was the vulnerability of Gosport where the fortifications were so ancient and so weak that once they were over-run, Portsmouth itself would be at the mercy of the invader. One writer put it, "A fleet sufficiently powerful to subdue any resistance it might find from ships at Spithead may take up any position it chooses between Cowes and Ryde without one single gun being brought to bear on it, either in taking up its position or when at anchor; and may then, with the certainty of smooth water, land its troops anywhere it pleases between Stokes Bay and Southampton Water", What would happen? "Once landed the first operation would be to occupy Fareham and throw up a series of lines from the harbour to the Solent, probably at Hill Head Haven; this done, and their left secure, their front being covered by the harbour, their rear by the sea and their fleet, they are at liberty to pursue operations against Gosport at leisure". The result would be inevitable—once in possession of Gosport, the dockyard and Portsmouth would be perfectly open. "The harbour, and all that it contains, may be destroyed". The government had erected two small works at Stokes Bay with 11 guns each but that was regarded as quite insufficient to hold a determined attack. The older fortifications of Gosport were so ineffective that they could not be expected to resist the invader for more than a few days. It was realised that if once an enemy occupied the Gosport-Fareham peninsular it would render Portsmouth and its harbour unusable. It might not be necessary for the foe to capture Portsmouth: it would become so untenable that it would have to be evacuated.

This was the nightmare that was so vivid to the strategists of the period and it is a situation which those of us who lived through the 1939-45 war can well understand. There were constant arguments as to the most effective means of defending the great naval base of Portsmouth. They all centred on two problems, one, providing a line of commanding forts on the hills running from Fareham to the north of Portsmouth, the other erecting adequate protection for Gosport itself against a sea-borne landing anywhere from Stokes Bay to Warsash. The former does not concern us here but the latter, when the plan was fully implemented, altered the whole character of Gosport.

The proposal that received most favour was to occupy the area stretching from Hardway or Elson's Hard across to Stokes Bay, a distance of some three miles, erecting three principal forts with moat defences and filling in with smaller defence works subsequently, so that a whole line of fortification some few miles out of the main town of Gosport would give determined resistance to any enemy landing in the Hillhead area. Stokes Bay itself was already partly covered by Fort Monckton, Gilkicker and the new fort at Stokes Bay and could be strengthened by a moat along the line of the beach. There were objections to these plans, particularly that the choice of Hardway or Elson would be too near the harbour and that the area to be covered was occupied by small villages (e.g. Brockhurst, Elson) gardens, farmhouses and lanes. Some declared that only a continuous line of fortifications would be adequate.

The scheme finally emerged, as do all such schemes, as a compromise. Between Fort Monckton and Gomer Ponds the moat was constructed, not as a major military canal which some advocated but as a deterrent to any invader. Fort Elson was proceeded with. Stokes Bay fort was strengthened and a new fort at Rowner was planned next and gradually the line of defencce, now familiar to us, in its decayed condition, stretching from Stokes Bay, Fort Gomer, Fort Rowner, Fort Brockhurst, on to Fort Elson began to emerge, the extent of the development representing the conflict between the military strategists, who considered the area the most vulnerable in the country and the Treasury which had to meet the cost. Within a few years of completion the whole position had changed, relations with France continued to improve, newer methods of defence rendered the older types of fortification useless and the whole system began to be regarded as a "folly". But in the 1850-60 period when the danger was real and imminent, these forts provided the first and major line of defence not merely for Portsmouth but for the whole country.

One result was to bound the growing Gosport area. The town had already outstripped the older line of ramparts which still remained around the old centre, and had spread into Forton, Newtown and even out towards Alverstoke. But Brockhurst and Elson provided the limit of the new growth. Beyond that came the ring of new fortifications and beyond that still, the far distant and quite separate villages at Rowner, Frater and Bedenham. During the 1914–18 war Fort Grange became the centre of the newly formed air force. Now the forts are there only in decay, the moats are being filled and houses have leaped over the fortifications to make Bridgemary, Rowner and Woodcot an integral part of Gosport. But when one examines them today, it is with the memory that only a hundred years ago when the defence line was being fashioned, it was considered the major safeguard against the loss of Portsmouth and its harbour, the destruction of the fleet and the conquest of the country.

Another result was the building of a new army barracks immediately outside the old ramparts. To form a basic reserve to defend the newly created line of forts at Browndown, Gomer, Rowner, Grange, Brockhurst and Elson it was decided to house a further regiment in Gosport and in 1859 the New Barracks (now known as St. George's Barracks) were erected at Clarence Road close to the Royal Clarence Yard. They were designed to be capable of housing 1,000 troops with their officers. An unconfirmed story, which arose from the architectural design of the barracks, declared that the plans for these premises were muddled with those for a new barracks to be erected in India, and that in Gosport there stands excellent accommodation for Indian conditions, while somewhere in India the barracks designed for Gosport were constructed.

The expansion in building work connected with the new fortifications and with the building of the new barracks largely accounted for the considerable increase in the population of the area during the decade 1850–1860.

CHAPTER 13

Gosport in the 1870's

In 1872 the Trustees for the purposes of the Acts of 1763 and 1815 for the watching, lighting and cleansing of the town of Gosport were still in existence. Their duties, for "the better paving of the streets and the preventing nuisances and other annoyances in the town of Gosport" still continued. By this period the problem of crossing the harbour was becoming even more important and this came under the heading of preventing nuisances. The watermen engaged in fierce rivalry for passengers, their boats rocked in the currents against the slimy, dangerous slipway as they shouted for custom. The time had arrived when some more efficient landing stage was urgently needed and when some organisation of the watermen both in their own interests and for the protection of those who had to make frequent journeys across the harbour, was essential. They found it neccessary, too, to unite together to combat the Floating Bridge.

The Trustees obtained Parliamentary powers in 1872 by the Pier and Harbour Orders Confirmation Act of that year, to construct "a wharf and pier or jetty at Gosport . . . and all necessary roads, approaches, sidings and other works and conveniences conneccted therewith, for the embarking and landing of passengers, fish, goods, coals, minerals, timber and merchandise, and for other purposes; which wharf, pier, jetty and landing-place shall commence from or near the sea wall, forming the high-water mark or line of ordinary spring tides at the eastern end of the High Street and Castle Row in Gosport and shall extend thence in an easterly direction into the harbour of Portsmouth, to a distance of 200 feet from the coping line of the proposed wharf wall, which coping line of wall shall be in a direct line from the steps at the north-east angle of Castle Row to the high-water mark of ordinary spring tides, on the land occupied by the Port of Portsmouth Floating Bridge Company".

The Trustees were given power to erect toll houses, landing stages and to dredge the harbour in the immediate area. They could demand payment in respect of persons, vessels, animals, fish, goods and other things in accordance with a schedule which varied from 1/8 for a ton of mahogany to ½d. for a bushel of apples. Marble tombstones were

93

exceptional and cost 5/- each so it didn't pay to buy one in Portsmouth for erection in Gosport.

About the same time, August 1875, the watermen joined together to form The Gosport and Portsea Watermen's Steam Launch Company. Nine master mariners from Gosport, Edward Sutton of Holly Street, James Batchelor of Chapel Row, William Knott of Castle Row, Joseph Christopher of South Street, Charles Hawkins of The Green, Jonathan Vincent of North Street, George Humby of Richard Street, Charles Smith of Clarence Square, John Grigg of North Street, joined with Henry Long, a Licensed Victualler of The Hard, Portsea to form a company to provide steam launches for the harbour crossing. The new company acquired in February 1876 four launches "Marquis of Lorne", "Princess Louise", "Lily" and "Grand Duchess", owned by promoters of the company and from that day onwards two companies have held a virtual monopoly of the harbour crossing and the local authority have had a control of the landing stage. At that time the local press was not enthusiastic about the scheme.

The Hampshire Telegraph for September 18th 1875 declared, "The report is revived that a new Steam Launch Company is about to be started which will have for its leading recommendation a half-penny tariff for the passage between the two shores. Of course the public would be very glad to see the fare between Gosport and Common Hard and Point reduced, and so far the venture would no doubt be hailed with satisfaction, but, as capitalists in this and neighbouring towns will be asked to assist to float a new enterprise, it is well that they should know exactly how the prospect of success is likely to be realised by a comparison with present results. The Floating Bridge Company was established 37 years ago, and with varying fortunes has run its conveyances for upwards of 35 years. It has, beside the two bridges, three admirably appointed launches and a 10 minutes communication is carried on uninterruptedly between Gosport and Portsmouth for 14 hours a day. The traffic is enormous, yet the expenses are so great that it pays only 5% to its shareholders. The Steam Launch Company is a younger venture which maintains a continuous passage of people between Gosport and Common Hard. The boats of the company are numerous and well-arranged, some of those working them being shareholders. As a rule the launches are at work about 17 hours a day— from 5.00 a.m. to 10.00 p.m.—yet as we hear the profits are barely 6% on the large outlay of capital and excessive hours of working. These are facts which capitalists should bear well in mind if the new company with a half-penny fare should be started".

All sorts of people crossed the harbour. William M. Thackeray, who spent some time at Bay House on the Solent Coast of Alverstoke, tells in the Book of Snobs of "Mademoiselle de Saugrenne, the interesting

94

young French woman with a profusion of pretty ringlets who lived for nothing at a boarding house at Gosport, was then conveyed to Fareham gratis; and being there and lying on the bed of the good old lady her entertainer, the dear girl took occasion to rip open the mattress and steal a cash-box with which she fled to London. How would you account for the prodigious benevolence shown towards the interesting young French lady? Was it her jetty ringlets or her charming face? Baa! Do ladies love others for having pretty faces and black hair? She said she was a relation of the Lord de Saugrenne; talked of her ladyship her aunt, and of herself as a de Saugrenne. The honest boarding house people were at her feet at once. Good, honest, simple, lord-loving children of Snobland". And who can blame them—for this was Gosport of the mid 19th century, poor folk of the small, backwater town, surrounded by the pomp and dignity of the Royal Navy. Gosport was the town the Queen passed through to Clarence Pier on her way to the Isle of Wight, the service station for the Royal Marines, the hospital and victualling centre for the Navy; Alverstoke was the home of retirement for the Senior Captains and the Admirals. All these comings and goings brought trade to the ferrymen.

The Royal Marines, housed at Forton Barracks since 1848, made a colourful adjunct to the life of Gosport. When the premises, "airy and elegant" as they were described, were handed over on 29th March, 1848, they were in fact in a shocking state of disrepair. Colonel Field described them as "by no means new having been used as a prison, a hospital, a place of confinement for French prisoners"—but he adds "They were a great improvement on the mean and cramped quarters they had occupied in Clarence Barracks". During the years after 1848 the barracks were widely developed. A good deal of the Forton Lake was reclaimed. The Millpond was bought from the Bishop of Winchester in 1858 for £775 and then reclaimed as a playing field. The process of reclamation cost more than thirteen times as much. Forton recreation field was added at a further cost of over £5,000. A school was built and later on, in 1893 a new theatre was completed which provided the Forton Theatrical Society with the opportunity of presenting fortnightly entertainment.

Among the people who used the ferry were the boys of Burney's Academy. The famous founder, Dr. William Burney, died in February 1822. He had been "Pious and steady, earnest in his religious duties, a truly affectionate and kind husband and parent; an upright Magistrate tempering justice with mercy, a patient and zealous preceptor; a most worthy and benevolent man" as the obituary notice ran. The pupils had other views about tempering justice with mercy for he was a martinet whose mercy wasn't apparent when he was executing justice with a cane. His son, Dr. Henry Burney, who had been in charge of the school for some years, carried on the same tradition. Several members of the Royal Family attended including the then Duke of Edinburgh, and Prince Louis of Battenburg. The school boasted the title "The Royal Academy". The national flag flew on the square before the school. By 1870 Dr. Edward Burney who had a preparatory school for younger boys at Bay House had become Headmaster.

Some of the most famous men in the navy were at the school in the second half of the 19th century. They included Admiral Togo (Commander in Chief of the Japanese navy) and Earl Beatty of Jutland. General Sir Sam Browne (of the Sam Browne belt fame) was also a pupil. The school passed out of the control of the Burney family in 1892 and finally moved to Shalford Park in Surrey in 1904. In 1907 another school, the first boys' school to be built by the the Urban District Council, was erected on the site.

Not all the people in Gosport were Royal Marines or boys of Burney's Academy. The wide-eyed boys were also at work. In 1875 there were many complaints that a large quantity of spurious 2/- coins were circulating in the town and tradesmen and residents were warned to be on their guard against counterfeits—particularly to examine the "milling" of the coins for the counterfeiters had been defeated in this part of the process. A particularly smart fellow did a sharp piece of swindling on Saturday, 11th September 1875. "He called at Mr. Vinson's shop and gave a large order for grocery goods, wishing them to be sent to an indicated house at Ann's Hill and added that he would take a bottle of the best port and also one of sherry with him, which could be included in the grocery account and be paid for when those goods were delivered. Being told that the rules of the establishment did not permit of such an arrangement, he left the shop and crossed to Mr. Foster's where the order was booked and the wine delivered. He next went to Mr. Cooke's and gave a large order taking with him a bottle of whiskey but before going far, he had the misfortune to break the bottle and returned for two more which were given him. The goods were duly despatched but no householder of the name given lived at Ann's Hill. The swindler has not yet been found. The three grocery and wine shops which he visited were within a space of thirty yards from each other. And there were quarrels among neighbours. Ann Brushwood was summoned for assaulting Josephine Hayward on the 11th September. Josephine was sitting in her back room in Henry Street during the evening when Ann came in. There was a wordy quarrel about the payment of some money during which "disgusting language was made use of by both parties". Josephine went into the yard whereupon Ann threw some dirty water over her on two occasions (although she told the court it was only one lot of dirty water). Ann was fined 8/- including costs—a huge sum for those days—but oh! the satisfaction.

Throughout her long reign from 1837 to 1901 Queen Victoria frequently visited (or at least passed through) Gosport. From the time of the establishment of the railway in 1841 the Queen used the Gosport line on her journeys to and from Osborne House. A link was made between Gosport Station and the Royal Clarence Yard where a small station was built close to the landing stage. The station had two waiting rooms, one for the Queen and her attendants and one for any distinguished company. The rooms were furnished from the stores at Clarence Yard on each occasion of a royal visit. The carpet was brought out to cover the distance from the royal railway coach to the Royal Yacht at the landing stage. There is a local story which tells how in October 1844 the Queen and the Prince Consort came to Gosport with Louis Phillipe who had been on a state visit. Louis was unable to embark owing to stormy weather and the Superintendent of the Royal Clarence Yard (Thomas T. Grant) was suddenly called upon to provide the royal party with a meal. Mr. Grant had guests at home but they were quietly sent away and the food intended for them was served to the Queen and her party. The Kentish Gazette on December 3rd 1844 reported, "It will be remembered that on the occasion of the departure of the King of France from this country, His Majesty and the Duke of Montpensier with the Queen and Prince Albert took refuge from the storm when about to embark at Gosport, in the house of T. T. Grant, Esq., the storekeeper of the Royal Clarence Victualling Yard, Gosport, where the most loyal, polite and delicate attention was rendered to this illustrious party by Mr. & Mrs. Grant. The Queen on several opportunities expressed her sense of those services but this week Her Majesty with the most gratifying condescension has been pleased to mark her estimation of Mr. Grant's conduct by presenting him with a most elegant piece of plate of great value". Later Mr. Grant also received a Knighthood for his services.

On 26th May, 1856, the Queen reviewed the 4th and 13th Light Dragoons at Royal Clarence Yard on their return from the Crimea and later that year she was invited to Browndown to inspect the German Legion encamped there. The visit in fact never took place. The German Legion turned out to be a riotous mob that caused havoc in the streets and pubs of Gosport.

St. Matthew's school, the largest and costliest school in Gosport, was just outside the Royal Clarence Yard where the railway cut through the town wall by the Forton Road gates and frequently the train was halted by Royal Command whilst the children of the school entertained her from their play ground with their physical exercises with dumb-bells and bar-bells and their school band of drums and fifes. The Queen would acknowledge these loyal greetings and the royal train would rumble on. The Prince of Wales visited Gosport even more frequently—but he came more quietly. Frequently after racing in the Royal Yacht "Britannia" at Cowes he would cross the Solent in a small boat, would land at Stokes Bay carried ashore on the back of a sailor and would join his convival friends at Bay House. This handsome building, designed in 1834 by Decimus Burton for the Baring banking family, is now the centrepiece of Bay House School. It occupies as good a site as any in the country, and adjoining is the parkland where a marvellous variety of trees and a delicate little cemetery for the pets of the family remind us of an elegant age gone by.

CHAPTER 14

Gosport—Local Government 1875-1895

One of the most interesting ways of studying the history of a town is to peruse the Minutes of its local government authority. It is fascinating to pry beyond the copperplate writing of the Clerk into the triumphs and disasters, the achievements and failures, the petty economies and the personal antagonisms of a bygone generation.

From 1875 to 1895, for a period of twenty years, the chief local government body in Gosport was the Alverstoke Local Board set up under the Public Health Acts 1875. Its offices were at Elliott Place in Stoke Road, outside the main town centre. These offices were used long before the new Town Hall and Thorngate Hall were erected. The years 1878-1879 show the kind of work undertaken by the Local Board and how different were the local government issues of that time, but how similar in many respects were the attitudes of the councillors to those of today.

At the Annual Meeting held on the 18th April, 1878, twenty members were present, and the Rev. Canon Walpole, Rector of Alverstoke, was unanimously appointed as Chairman. Four Committees were established: Road and Works, Sanitary, Finance, and General Purposes.

Almost the first problem which engaged the attention of the Board was the need to raise a loan to pay for road repairs and improvements and it was resolved to borrow £1,000 from the South Western Branch of the Ancient Order of Foresters, to be repaid in 15 years at 4½% interest. Having completed that transaction the Board proceeded to increase the salary of the Collector of Rates to the princely total of £100 a year.

Borough Councillors of today who know the pattern of these things will not be surprised that the Collector of Rates having got his increase, applications were received forthwith from the Surveyor and the Clerk. There were furious arguments with proposals, counter proposals, resolutions, amendments, threats and innuendoes. It was finally resolved that the Surveyor should receive an increase from £150 to £200 a year but "that the salary of the Clerk be not increased".

The Board had its own back on the Surveyor for shortly afterwards it passed two solemn resolutions: 1. That they had considered an Estimate from the Surveyor for a new rate which being deemed excessive he had been requested to reconsider with a view to reduction; 2. That they had instructed the Surveyor not to be extravagant in the use of road materials.

Indeed financial restrictions seemed to be dominant in the minds of members of the Board. They reported that they had ordered the purchase of a cob and a cart to stand over for the present. In February 1879 came another example of care in expenditure. "The Brockhurst drainage scheme", runs the Minute, "being adjourned from October, it was resolved to recommend that the question stand over until the finances of the Board are in a more flourishing condition".

And how serious was the financial position? In June 1878 the Board considered its budget for the next half year. It estimated to spend a total of £3,915, including lighting £123; scavenging £70; road watering £368; highway maintenance £1,008; drainage £150 and salaries £326. It proposed to raise the money by a general district rate of 1/2 in the £1 which would produce £3,090.

Much of the discussion of the Board concerned the sanitary arrangements of the town which were in a parlous condition and at almost every meeting of the Sanitary Committee complaints were made against over-filled cesspits and privies. The town drains were few and overflowing. A proposal that permission be given to the proprietors of the Market House to connect their cesspit in the Market House with the main drain in Market Row was defeated. The Medical Officer reported that he had inspected the drain at the top of High Street "which empties itself into Gosport Moat the outlet of which is very offensive" and had "left the matter in the hands of the Surveyor"—at least that is how the Minute reports the incident.

There was serious concern about the condition of the moats. The Board received a report that because of the offensive state of the moats at Gosport and Stokes Bay the Inspector of Nuisances had been instructed to call upon the Commanding Officer of Engineers to request that a greater amount of flushing might be done. The Inspector's demands were not complied with and we read, "That the Chairman, Mr. Burney and Mr. Coulter do wait as a deputation on the Commanding Officer of Engineers to urge more frequent flushing of the moats at Gosport and Alverstoke".

Mr. Millidge was ordered to cleanse and purify the water of his well at Ann's Hill or provide other good supply. The Inspector was directed "to remove and disinfect all sewage matter or earth unduly saturated with filth promptly". No wonder the death rate was high. In August 1878 no fewer than 13 babies died of diarrhoea, and typhoid fever was epidemic in Queens Road.

Some of the items considered by the Local Board illustrate some of the problems of the period. A special sub-Committee was appointed on the subject of bathing at Stokes Bay. It reported that the sub-Committee had viewed the spot and determined that notice-boards be fixed restricting the public from bathing within 75 yards eastward from Stokes Bay Railway pier; within 100 yards westward of the Bathing machines, and near the coast guard hut. There were furious arguments about the desirability of permitting public bathing at all.

The Board appointed a special deputation to wait upon Colonel Shaw with a view to obtaining some further information as to throwing open the double gateway (of the gates at Mumby Road) for the greater safety of foot and carriage traffic. Only the side gates were opened.

But new-fangled notions were abroad and during the year a great deal of attention was given by the Board to a Bill in Parliament to construct a tramway from Gosport to Alverstoke and to Brockhurst. Modern times were coming with a rush.

Finally, as in later generations, the toll bridge at Haslar was causing trouble. The Board had a remedy to suggest as is shown in the following resolution: "That as the Admiralty contemplate erecting additional sheds at Haslar, application be made to them to take over the Haslar toll bridge and throw the same open to the public free from toll".

The Minutes of the Gosport Borough Council for the 20th October 1958 recorded that in November 1956 the council resolved to approve the acquisition and reconstruction of the Haslar Toll Bridge at a total estimated cost of £119,834 of which £63,797 would be contributed by the Council and £56,037 by the Admiralty. The Minute authorised the purchase of the bridge and the preparation of plans for its reconstruction.

Ever since the building of Haslar Hospital, the problem of access across the Haslar Creek to avoid a long detour through Alverstoke and Clayhall has been under consideration. A little ferry carried passengers across but heavy goods had to be taken by road. In April 1791 a grant was made to Mr. Forbes, a merchant of Gosport for the "liberty of building a bridge for which he is to have a certain toll and it being a considerable thoroughfare will be found more convenient than the usual mode of ferrying over". The bridge was to be built of wood and brick and was to cross Stoke Lake, as it was called, from the Royal Hospital at Haslar "to the Windmill opposite on the Gosport side". The bridge was duly constructed and became known locally as Forbes Bridge. In 1801 the bridge was destroyed under circumstances about which we can only speculate. Forbes now began a long battle with the Admiralty for compensation for the loss of his livelihood. A temporary wooden bridge was put up by the Royal Engineers in 1811, but this collapsed three years later. Nothing further was done until 1834 when Robert Cruikshank, the developer responsible for many of Gosport's building projects, formed a company to build a new road bridge over the Creek. In 1835 this was completed, the Admiralty agreeing to pay £50 per annum to the Bridge Company in consideration that officers and staff of the Hospital should be exempt from tolls.

During the middle period of the 19th century when the army fortification against French invasion was strengthened at Gilkicker and Fort Monckton the bridge became an important means of communication.

It was in January 1879 that Mr. Whitecombe proposed to the Local Board that the Admiralty should be asked, since it was erecting additional sheds at the hospital, to take over the bridge and throw it open to the public free from tolls. There was a long discussion and finally in March 1879 a sub-Committee was appointed "to feel their way" (as the Minute said) "with the Admiralty and the War Department".

The sub-Committee duly felt their way and they reported back to the Local Board in May 1879. This was their report.

"Your Committee beg to report with regard to the purchase of Haslar Bridge and the freeing it from toll that they here had an interview with the proprietors of the bridge and ascertained that the average income from the tolls free of all expenses has been during the last 10 years nearly £600 per annum which at 5% represents a sum of nearly £12,000. The proprietors however are willing to sell the bridge for £10,000 to meet in some degree the interests of the public.

"Your Committee have also seen His Serene Highness Prince Edward of Saxe Weimar the Lieutenant General commanding the Southern District, Colonel Jervis, R.E. Commanding Royal Engineers and Colonel Shaw, R.E. Commanding the Gosport Division. Captain Balliston (a member of the Committee) has also spoken to the First Lord of the Admiralty on the subject.

"Your Committee are glad to be able to report that all these authorities received the proposal to free the bridge from toll most favourably. No definite terms however were prepared and your Committee would now ask that you should authorise them to make the following proposal viz.: The Alverstoke Local Board, with the consent of the Local Government Board, to contribute the sum of £2,000, the War Department £3,000 and the Admiralty £5,000, or that without mentioning the respective sums that the War Department and the Admiralty should contribute, the Alverstoke Local Board should give £2,000 and the remainder of the purchase money be found by their Departments and the bridge to become their property on the condition that it should be free of toll for ever afterwards".

Alas, the best laid schemes of men sometimes fail and the project fell through. The Cruikshank bridge remained in situ until 1940 when the Admiralty removed the centre span to allow easier access to Gunboat Yard. A temporary high-level footbridge was erected to cover the missing section and the structure was popularly known as 'Pneumonia Bridge'—presumably because in winter months any patients en route to Haslar Hospital would have pneumonia added to their symptoms by the time they had braved the elements attacking the windswept bridge!

In February 1889 the question of providing a public library in Gosport was under consideration. The Local Board in 1889 made the first move towards establishing a library by including in the rate estimate for the half year ending 29th September, 1889, an item of £256 for the establishment of a public library. Progress was slow and when it came to the next half year ending 25th March, 1890, nothing was included for libraries—the rate had to be kept down to 1/3 in the £ for the half year. But by January 1890 a Library Committee had been established and presented its first report. They contemplated the purchase of 1 High Street, Gosport which had been offered to them for £1,100 but, as the Report says "considering the state of the library funds and insufficiency of the size of the house offered, they were unable to accept the proposal. They also turned down 7 High Street offered at £800. But they did recommend that a strip of land at the rear of High Street and the then new Thorngate Hall be accepted on a rental basis as a site for a temporary Free Public Library. They also reported that they had purchased from Messrs. Bull and Son of Southampton at a cost of £25 a wooden building previously at the rear of the Naval Club in Portsmouth to be used as a temporary library. The lowest tender for the removal of the second-hand timber hut from Portsmouth to Gosport and for its re-erection was £54 18s. 11d.

So a start was made in a second-hand hut to establish a library for Gosport. Significantly enough by June, 1890, when the actual bill had to be paid, the cost of the work had risen to £81 12s. 7d. showing that it is always unsatisfactory to buy second-hand timber buildings. The Committee inspected the building but the main feature that troubled them was the position of the urinal and they resolved to recommend that a door be placed on the outside of the urinal and hinged to the corner of the library.

A tender of £160 was accepted for building a reading room. But the Committee realised that their temporary arrangements would not be satisfactory for long and they instructed a Surveyor to prepare plans for a proper library. Another ten years was to lapse before the plans came to anything.

The Library Committee began to work out the details of the organisation of this important service. In July 1890 they determined on the times of opening which were to be from 11 a.m. to 1 p.m.; 3 p.m. to 5 p.m. and from 6 p.m. to 9.30 p.m. Then came the vitally important problem of staff. They decided that a librarian should be appointed at a salary of £1 per week, and that two female assistants should be employed at 4/- per week. Did they get an applicant for the post of librarian at £1 a week? Of course they did—there were seven at least and they finally appointed a Royal Naval Pensioner, Mr. Benjamin Carter, of Stamshaw. He commenced duties on the 22nd September 1890.

There were generous donors to the newly formed library. The Minutes of the Local Board record with appreciation a gift of £50 for the purchase of books. The donor was Mr. T. N. Blake. They were also given a satin walnut bookcase. The Vicar of Elson also presented 23 volumes. But other equipment had to be purchased and orders were placed for library fittings at £30 10s. 6d. for tables at 45/- each and chairs at 5/2 a time. It was decided that all books should be purchased from a local bookseller Mr. Walford, and that the library should be known as the Gosport and Alverstoke Free Public Library.

By December 1890 the Library Committee was hard at work. They instructed the librarian to purchase books of reference. An Encyclopaedia Britannica bound in half Russian leather at 36/- per volume was ordered together with Blackie's "Imperial Gazeteer". They gave directions for a porch to be erected inside the reading room and to meet the rigours of winter they ordered two stoves—one for the library and one for the reading room.

But it was on the 12th of February 1891 that the library came into its own. The Library Committee reported to the Local Board that they had ordered mats, a dial clock, fittings for newspaper desks, an umbrella stand, two gas brackets and a screen. The Minutes of the Local Board for 12th February 1891 end with these words, "At this stage of the meeting the Chairman announced his intention of formally opening the Free Public Library and at his invitation the members (18 of them) adjourned to the library when the Chairman performed the opening ceremony in the presence of the whole of the members and others after which the members returned to the Board Room and filled up the necessary forms for the borrowing of books and drank success to the Free Public Library amid hearty cheers. The drinking of the Chairman's health brought the interesting ceremony to a close".

We don't know whether the members used their tickets to borrow books, but as to the drinking of toasts—well, the Chairman of the Local Board, Colonel Mumby, was a prominent local manufacturer of mineral water.

So began Gosport's first library—in a second-hand timber hut. Within another ten years a much more imposing edifice was to be erected in Walpole Road which would remain the town's library until 1973 when it became the Gosport Museum.

CHAPTER 15

Gosport or Alverstoke
or Alverstoke and Gosport

It was in November 1890 when preparations were being made for the 1891 Census that the officials noticed a curious fact. Whereas all the records and returns made by the Registrar General since 1851 were under the name of Gosport, the local urban sanitary authority was called the Alverstoke Local Board. It was decided to write to the Local Board about it.

If the official who drafted the letter had realised the storm of controversy that it would arouse, he would probably have 'forgotten' to post it. Alverstoke had a proud name going back to Domesday and beyond and claimed the ancient rights of a medieval church and immemorial charters. More recently it had become the home of retired (but by no means retiring) senior officers of the fleet. Gosport on the other hand had a murky past and a doubtful present. Its oldest church only went back to 1696; it was merely a collection of hovels at the time when Alverstoke was a prosperous village. Its ancient charters were legendary and possibly never existed. It had grown rapidly as a result of the French wars of the 18th century, but hemmed in by ramparts and fortifications it was insular in outlook and, as we have seen, unsavoury in sanitation. But if it hadn't the area and the wealth of Alverstoke it certainly had a far greater (the people of Alverstoke said a far denser) population. The official who passed the letter knew none of these things. He was merely inquisitive.

Never was there such a furore in a small town. When the innocent enquiry came before the Alverstoke Local Board on the 11th December 1890 one of the members immediately gave notice that at the very next meeting he would submit a motion concerning the name of the Authority—what he really meant was a notice to change the same.

So when the members assembled for their monthly meeting on the 8th January 1891 it was with hushed expectancy. The season of goodwill having passed, the new year having been ushered in (with its arrangements for the census) the Local Board prepared to do battle. It was a civil war between the Gosportians, many in numbers, raucous in demands and blatant in their claims that the majority must have its right, and the Alverstocracy, zealous of its inheritance, pugnacious in defence of privilege and resolved to retain its proud name.

The first round of the contest went to the Gosportians. On their behalf Mr. Blake moved and Dr. Kealy seconded that application be made to the Local Government Board for permission "to change the name of this authority from Alverstoke to Gosport". The members from the Gosport wards were clearly in a majority and able to dominate the proceedings. After a long debate two members sounded a note of caution and suggested as a compromise that the name should be the Gosport and Alverstoke Local Board. The Gosportians would have none of it and the amendment was defeated by 15 votes to 4. Then amid triumphal applause the resolution for the change of name was adopted by 15 votes to 3 and duly dispatched to the Local Government Board in London.

But that was only the beginning of the battle. The Gosportians, over-confident in their majority on the Local Board, had reckoned without the resourcefulness and pugnacity of the men of Alverstoke led by the redoubtable Admiral Field, M.P. Letters, which might have been written in vitriol, appeared in the press. Meetings, agitations, deputations, abuse, innuendoes, poured out from Alverstoke. The name that went back to Saxon times was not to be changed on the enquiry of an officious clerk in the Registrar General's office. This place had been known as Alverstoke long before the name Gosport was dreamed of, and they would see that it remained as Alverstoke for ever.

By March, 1891, the storm had hit the Local Government Board in its usually quiet haven in Whitehall. The dignified Civil Servants there, concerned at the violence of the passions aroused, sent down a soothing letter suggesting that "Alverstoke and Gosport" might be a compromise solution acceptable to all parties.

But by this time the fury and abuse from Alverstoke had aroused the ire of the men of Gosport who after all had a majority in the Local Board. Gosport it must be, they determined, and nothing else. At the meeting on the 12th March, 1891, the whole issue was raised in the strongest possible terms. One can almost feel the iron claw behind the velvet glove of the resolution submitted. "While acknowledging the courteous reply from the Local Government Board respecting the change of name of this authority", it read, "we must respectfully decline to accept the suggested alteration to Alverstoke and Gosport or any suggested alteration that entails plurality of names. The Board therefore press their claim upon the Local Government Board and express the hope that consent will not be withheld to their request. Should, however, any adverse decision be contemplated they pray that the Local Government Board will cause a public enquiry to be held by one of their Inspectors so as to enable the Board to submit their arguments in greater detail and give to the memorialists an opportunity of stating their case fully". Amendments to accept "Gosport and Alverstoke" or "Alverstoke and Gosport" were brushed aside and the main resolution passed by 14 votes against 4. The Gosportians had won the second round.

The fury rose all the more, with charges and counter charges, threats and demands, personalities and abuse until at last the Local Government Board took the hint and determined that Colonel John Ord Hasted, R.E. should hold a local public enquiry. Bills appeared round the town stating, "Whereas the Local Board of the district of Alverstoke have applied to the Local Government Board for sanction to change their name from the 'Alverstoke Local Board' to the 'Gosport Local Board' the Local Government Board have directed that inquiry be made into the subject matter of such application, etc".

When Colonel Hasted arrived on the scene to conduct the enquiry on Tuesday 7th April, 1891, he was confronted with the rival and angry contestants, at least 68 of them, all trying with their followers to crowd into the smallish committee chamber. It was impossible to proceed in the overcrowded room and in such a tense atmosphere. Finally the enquiry was adjourned to the nearby Thorngate Hall which had been erected only a few years before. There, before the Inspector, before their 68 friends and rivals, and indeed before the public of Gosport and Alverstoke they argued out their claims. Eight members testified to support the case of the Local Board for the name Gosport and eight including the redoubtable Admiral Field, M.P. and Colonel Longmore urged the claims of Alverstoke. Hectic were the arguments, violent the abuse, passionate the appeals. The Inspector was confronted with the forthright language of Admirals at bay and the insistence of local dignitaries conscious of their majority.

But as the day wore on tempers began to calm, the Admirals began to regret the civil war and those from Gosport to appreciate the personal worth of retired admirals as well as their contribution to the rates. The Inspector helped a great deal and finally over the troubled water both the men of Gosport and the men of Alverstoke sailed together into a haven of compromise with flags flying.

Two days later the Local Board met again—and the record runs "The Chairman having stated the result of the public enquiry held with reference to the change in the name of the Board, it was moved and seconded 'That in consequence of opinion at the public enquiry held last Tuesday the Board amend the application to the Local Government Board dated 8th January 1891 by asking that the name of the Alverstoke Local Board be changed to the Gosport and Alverstoke

Local Board'. Carried unanimously"—and it was so.

In 1894 a new Local Government Act established the Urban District Councils, and Gosport became the Gosport and Alverstoke U.D.C.

The first meeting of the new Council was held on Thursday, 3rd January, 1895, when 26 of the 27 newly elected Councillors attended. They had been elected, at a cost of £167 10s. 2d., in three wards—the Gosport Ward, the South Ward and the North Ward, each with nine members. They set about their administrative business with a will. Dr. John Kealy was unanimously elected as Chairman; it was agreed that the three members of each ward with the lowest votes should retire in April 1896, those three with the next lowest in April 1897 and those with the highest votes, in April 1898. Committees were established and Standing Orders to govern the conduct of business were worked out.

One of the very first problems was how to find enough room for members of the general public who wished to attend, an issue which still remained sixty years later on. One suggestion was that each member should be permitted to invite one person to the Council meeting but this was rejected partly because it would have made the Council room too congested and partly because it meant buying 27 chairs. So a compromise was reached to purchase 18 chairs to permit the first 18 persons applying to have the good fortune to listen to their Councillors debating. Even this involved cutting the table in the Council room in two and widening each side as well as accommodating some members at desks at the back. The chairs cost 8/6 each. Judge of the fury of some of the members when they arrived to the next meeting in April, 1895, only to find that the alterations had not been made and the general public was still excluded. Mr. Sandford demanded to know by what right the public was excluded. There was a violent storm of argument until finally a resolution was passed, "That seeing the Council Room is not in a fit conditon to receive the public, the public be not admitted to this meeting". It never has been until this day fit for the comfort of the public, but those who desire to attend have at least the comfort of knowing the discomforts experienced by their predecessors.

The weather in January and February, 1895, was bitterly cold and is reflected in the following Minute. "Your Committee instructed the Clerk to write to the Water Company asking them to allow their hydrants and standpipes throughout the district to be used at certain hours throughout the day for domestic purposes as many houses, through the severe frost, are without water supply". Talking of water supply it is significant to note that the Council decided that the water in Forton Creek was not wholesome enough even for watering the streets and later on arrangements were made to water the roads with sea water

110

because the Water Company couldn't supply enough for the purpose.

Then, as now, the problem of salaries and wages to be paid to Council officials was a matter of great concern and lengthy argument. In January, 1895, Mr. Carter, who had been librarian since the inception of the public library, decided to take another appointment at Kingston-on-Thames. His service had been most valuable and the Council resolved to express their full appreciation of the very excellent manner in which he had carried out his work. But they then proceeded to promote the Assistant Librarian as Librarian. And the salary—£1 per week, rising by increments of 2/6 a year to a maximum of 30/- a week. This of course left the post of Assistant Librarian open and after considering nine applications it was resolved to appoint Mr. A. I. Liddle at a commencing salary of 5/- a week, rising to 7/6 after one year's service and to a maximum of 10/- a week after two years' service.

When a junior assistant was appointed to the surveyor's office the salary was again 5/- per week, rising to a maximum of 10/-. An amendment to make the basic rate of 6/- a week was defeated. Similarly an attempt to increase the salary of the Assistant Surveyor from £65 to £80 a year was held up for some months.

After that came the problems of settling the wages of the labourers. In April, 1895, Mr. Hodgson moved: "That the Gosport and Alverstoke Urban District Council increase the pay of their employees to minimum as set forth: Foreman of labourers 8½d. per hour; men of all trades 8d. per hour; skilled labourers 6d. per hour; ordinary labourers 5½d. per hour; indifferent labourers 5d. per hour; and the hours of labour be reduced to 48 per week. All this represented a considerable improvement upon the prevailing rates.

After Mr. Hooley had spoken at some length in support of the proposal the whole matter was adjourned for a fortnight. When it was resumed, there was a fierce debate. Some agreed that Gosport rates compared favourably with those paid in Portsmouth and in the Dockyard, that the current market rate was the right standard to adopt, some complained about the standard of work of Council employees. In the end the matter was referred back to a Sub-Committee to make further enquiries. A month later the Sub-Committee came back with a recommendation that the minimum rates of wages for unskilled labourers should be 18/- a week and for skilled labourers 20/- a week. An attempt to get better terms was turned down. And, as if to emphasise that the workman must be worthy of his hire, a resolution was passed that "if in the opinion of the Surveyor any man is found to be not competent, dilatory or negligent he be discharged".

But of course prices were very different during the early months of

1895 from what they are today. Good class houses could be rented for less than £20 a year (i.e. less than 7/6 a week inclusive), coal was £1 a ton with a reduction from prompt payment. Tea cost 1/- a pound, the very best butter 10d. a pound. You could buy a new piano for £19 (or 10/6 a month) and Messrs. Blakes of Gosport advertised their celebrated Haslar Ale at 2/6 for a dozen pints. Ordinary ale and stout cost 1/- per gallon. The Council budgeted in March, 1895, to spend £5,523 during the half year on all its services and this required a rate of 1/4 in the pound for the half year.

Before the new Urban District Council had been functioning six months it was confronted with a very serious problem concerning the drainage of the town. Even in 1600 and before there are references to the noisome and pestiferous condition of the drains, and by 1761 conditions had become so bad that the first body of Commissioners was appointed to clear up the open gully drains. By 1814 the situation had again become so unsatisfactory that a further Act of Parliament was secured and a new body of Commissioners appointed. They too were singularly ineffective.

By 1851 the population was 16,353 and was increasing fairly rapidly. Over 7,000 still lived within the ramparts in closely packed alleyways and courtyards. It was reported in 1851 that there were 104 courtyards and alleyways within the walled town and in them some 750 densely populated tenement houses. Local Government was difficult in any case. The 33 trustees who formed the Local Branch were self-elected, the Highway Authority was elected by the Vestry, and any reasonable system of sanitation from such bodies was extremely unlikely. The cesspit system was exclusively in vogue. Cesspits were dug and allowed to fill until they became so foul that another had to be dug nearby. Since most of the water came from local wells the results can be imagined.

Gradually improved methods had to be adopted. In the newer houses being constructed at the rate of about 100 a year outside the ramparts, earth closets (the so-called pan system) were used and night carts were engaged to carry the filth and muck to the creeks, to Stokes Bay or to the upper reaches of the harbour. There were constant complaints from the residents of the newer part of Alverstoke about the noise and offensiveness of the wagons which rumbled through the streets at night on their necessary but nasty duty. But the problem was growing more serious. By 1891 the population had increased to 25,457 and sanitary conditions were again becoming rather dreadful if not disgusting.

The inhabitants didn't worry very much. In 1866 the parish was polled on the subject of a main drainage scheme, but while 623 voted for, 1,007 voted against, and as a result the majority of 384 had their

112

way and the general principle of drainage remained that of cesspits gradually being replaced by earth closets. It is almost unbelievable that less that 80 years ago the "Portsmouth Times" could assert "our figures will go to prove that the health of the neighbourhood can be maintained and improved with a better and more improved earth closets system as well as by any arterial (i.e. water borne) method of drainage". The paper went on, in the way journalists, and sometimes Councillors do, to deride the theorists and support the practical men. "We have positive proof before us" (of the virtues of earth closet drainage) "while the best that scientists can give us is the theory that modern sanitation with water carriage will further improve the health of the district".

The bombshell burst on 20th August 1895 in the form of a letter from the Local Government Board (the central body in charge of local government). The letter was perhaps the most shocking ever received by the local urban sanitary authority of Gosport and Alverstoke, and it immediately caused consternation and violent controversy. It is worth quoting in full. "I am directed by the Local Government Board to transmit to you the enclosed extract from a letter which the Board have received from the Lords Commissioners of the Admiralty with reference to the conditions of the west side of Portsmouth Harbour. The Board request that they may receive the observations of the Urban District Council of Gosport and Alverstoke upon the matters dealt with therein". The letter enclosed was as follows. "I am commanded by the Lords Commissioners of the Admiralty to place before you, for the information and consideration of the Local Government Board the following particulars as to the present condition of the foreshores, etc., on the west side of Portsmouth Harbour in reference of the general question of the drainage of the district of Gosport. For a considerable time past the attention of the Admiralty has been directed to the insanitary condition of the mud banks and of the various creeks which run into the harbour on the Gosport side. This is caused by sewage being discharged into these creeks whence it is deposited upon the banks and foreshores. Such conditions arise from the fact that the Gosport and Alverstoke Local Board have no adequate system of drainage. To a certain extent the sewage is disposed of by means of cesspits and earth closets, but it is impossible to prevent a considerable amount of objectionable matter from finding its way into the harbour. So far as the Government Establishments are concerned their drainage is mainly into the harbour direct. The condition of these banks and foreshores is getting worse from year to year and as Gosport and the surrounding neighbourhood is extending the matter is becoming gradually more serious. It is desirable from a sanitary point of view that steps should be undertaken to provide an adequate system of drainage for the whole of the district. The proper discharge of such a system would doubtless be into the Solent and thereby Portsmouth Harbour would be practically freed from the discharge into it of sewage matter. The Admiralty and War Department have been in correspondence on the matter and they are of the opinion that such a scheme should be undertaken".

On 17th September 1895, the council resolved to turn the tables on the government departments. After long and earnest consideration they resolved, "That this Council having duly considered the letter from the Admiralty are of the opinion that it is not the drainage caused by the civilian population of Gosport and Alverstoke that is polluting the mudbanks and foreshores on the west side of Portsmouth Harbour but that which is thrown into the adjacent creeks from government establishments or buildings or neighbouring houses. The Council feel, however, that further consideration of the subject might be advanced if representatives of the Admiralty, War Department and Local Government Board conferred with the Council". That was a clear denial of responsiblity but a willingness to accept any financial aid that might be forthcoming.

The arguments about the liability for the drainage system, the responsibility of the service departments and the most effective and efficient method of drainage went on for another nine months. In April 1896 the Local Government Board indicated that it had reached the stage where it was about to appoint a deputation to wait upon the Council. Meanwhile conditions weren't getting any better. In December 1895 the Surveyor reported that he had discovered that overflow cesspits in Linden Grove, Alverstoke were connected with a drain whose outfall was on the foreshore of Workhouse Creek. The owners claimed ignorance and the Surveyor was instructed to "use the greatest vigilance" in seeing that the houses were disconnected. Nor was the emptying of earth closets a cheap way out of the difficulty. In June, 1896, some members tried to throw the burden of the cost of this foulsome task upon the occupiers of houses, but the Clerk reported that it was the duty of the Local Authority to provide proper and efficient means of sewerage and that since the majority of the earth closets owners had been induced to provide their closets on the undertaking that the authority would empty them, the Council were unable legally or morally to make a charge for emptying them.

Finally it was announced that a full conference with representatives from the Admiralty, the War Office and the Local Government Board as well as the Councillors themselves would be held on the 20th June, 1896, to examine the whole problem of sanitation. To arm themselves for the fray and to appoint their delegates the Urban District Councillors met in private and special session two days before—i.e. on the 18th June, 1896. There was a prolonged and anxious debate in which most of the members of the Council took part. The main topic was whether a completely new drainage system was required. Finally a vote was taken on the question, "Is a complete system of arterial (water borne) drainage for this district desirable?". One voted in favour of the proposal and twelve against. There were 16 present. As a result six members were appointed to be a committee to express the views of the Council against the adoption of a scheme of arterial drainage.

On Saturday 20th June, 1896, the Conference on the drainage of Gosport was duly held. Colonel Hasted represented the Local Government Board and presided. There were three officials from the War Office and one from the Admiralty. On behalf of the Council Mr. George Cooke explained the difficulties of providing a completely new water borne drainage system in a scattered district with a low rateable value. He declared that the government departments were themselves the major culprits. But the main point made by the local representatives was that the financial position of the Council was such as to militate against any large outlay. They just couldn't afford it. The government departments met this difficulty by promising to contribute a capital sum towards the cost of any approved project in proportion to their rateable value. Then came an argument as to whether drainage under any new scheme should be into the harbour or into the Solent. Colonel Hasted declared that if the effluent should be discharged into the harbour certain treatment would be required but if into the Solent a much more modified treatment would suffice. Major Rablan representing the Admiralty made it quite clear that if sewage were to be discharged into the harbour it must be rendered perfectly innocuous.

So for the first time the minds of the Councillors began to turn to the idea of dumping sewage into the Solent. The conference ended on a pleasant note, the Admiralty and War Office representatives expressed their desire to come to a friendly arrangement which would abate the worst of the nuisances.

A few days later—on July 2nd—the Council met again in private to consider what should be done in view of the information given at the Conference. Again there was a full and somewhat heated discussion in which practically all the members took part. Finally it was decided in view of the offer by the Admiralty and War Office to make a contribution towards the cost, that an expert sanitary engineer should be consulted to give advice as to whether the existing arrangements could be improved upon by some method of treatment of sewage material or whether a scheme could be devised to cover a part of the area, and, of course, what would be the cost. A special committee called "The Drainage Committee" was appointed to receive and study the report".

It was in September that the Drainage Committee reported that they had appointed a consultant firm of sanitary engineers to prepare a scheme in sufficient detail for submission to the Service departments. That was by no means the end of the story. A complete scheme of drainage could not be cheap and Gosport was not wealthy. The battle between cost and effective drainage went on into the next century until at last under the threat of refusal by the Service departments to contribute towards the cost of local sanitary services the Council was finally forced into action.

CHAPTER 16

A Town Growing Up

In addition to the problem of providing an effective main drainage system, the Gosport and Alverstoke Urban District Council found itself confronted with a host of serious issues in the last few years of the 19th Century.

One of these concerned the arrangements for protection from fire.

Today we are used to a highly organised, extremely efficient County fire-fighting service equipped with the most up to date apparatus and staffed by proficient professional officers with special training for this work.

But in 1897 it was debatable whether the fire service should be a completely voluntary organisation of enthusiastic amateur firemen giving their service and often lending their equipment when occasion demanded or whether the local Urban District Council should take over.

Had you lived in Gosport then you would have been aware of the acute controversy. Many people argued that it was wrong to put the fire service on the rates when there were volunteers willing and able to meet the requirements. Others asserted that the risks in modern times were too great to leave fire protection to the amateur firemen however keen they might be.

Finally, on the 14th October, 1897, the advocates of the new order won the day and the Urban District Council resolved to take over the affairs of the Volunteer Gosport and Alverstoke Fire Brigade and to appoint a Committee to manage the new local government service.

But of course, in the good English way, there is always a compromise in matters of this kind. The Committee interviewed Mr. Mortimore the Superintendent of the old Volunteer Fire Brigade and appointed him as the Superintendent of the new Urban District Brigade at a salary of £5 per annum. They then interviewed Mr. Legg (the Secretary of the old Volunteer brigade) and appointed him as Assistant Superintendent at a salary of £3 per year. For the rest it was agreed that the other members of the old brigade be appointed as Firemen and be paid a retaining fee of £1 a year plus 1/- for each fire drill attended. But they were being very cautious and not slinging the ratepayers' money around for they stipulated that the number of drills be limited to twelve in any one year. And as a business Council they decided to acquire the whole of the appliances of the late fire brigade at a total inclusive cost of £25.

Having become responsible for the Fire Brigade, the Council determined to have a parade and on the 13th November all the firemen with all the £25's worth of equipment turned out in force at Clarence Square. There was a formal drill followed by a test of the gear. Such an overhaul was necessary because only a few weeks before there had been a quite serious fire at the Anglesey Hotel.

As with every inspection, deficiencies were found. What could you expect for £25?. Extra fire hose had to be ordered. The fire escape ladder needed repainting and revarnishing and that cost £4. The fire station was in a dreadful condition. It was let to one of the firemen at 3/- a week. An estimate of £1 12s. 6d was accepted to repaper the Committee room and the fire station itself and to clean and revarnish all the woodwork.

The Committee found themselves confronted with demands for new expenditure, and some of them complained bitterly of the new extravagances involved in running a Council Fire Brigade. Someone had to clean the gear and appliances—and who should it be but the Superintendent, and he was granted £8 a year for the work. Then if you have a Council Fire Brigade its chief officers must be suitably accoutred. And so £10 had to be spent on one helmet (nickel plated) one waist belt, one axe-in-case for the Superintendent. The Assistant Superintendent had to have the same, except that his helmet was of brass. Waterproof firemen's boots were expensive. They cost 27/- a pair—a quite outrageous price. But like good employers the Committee agreed that the Committee room over the fire station should be used as a social club room by members of the Brigade. Even by the end of the century—in 1899—the estimated cost of the whole fire service, staff, equipment, appliances, the lot was £120 for the whole year.

Although the fire brigade depended upon hired horses and part time services it could be very prompt when there was an emergency. On the 22nd of September, 1898, a fire broke out on the Stokes Bay line at 11.45 a.m. The alarm was received at Gosport at 12 noon and by 12.15 p.m. the Superintendent and four men with appliances arrived on the scene. But by that time the fire was out. It was a good job that the outbreak didn't occur on the 8th November because on that day the Superintendent and four firemen went to London at an inclusive cost to the Council of £4 5s. 0d. to attend a demonstration lecture on fire extinguishing. It might be argued that this looks expensive. But on the day following the lecture (a lecture, by the way, during which there were strong objections to stone staircases and too much iron work in buildings) the firemen from Gosport took part in the Lord Mayor's Show and were complimented for their smart and well set-up appearance and the able manner in which they carried out their duties. Who, after this, would begrudge them the dinner they had at the Holborn Restaurant or would think it amiss that they didn't arrive home in Gosport until 10.15 p.m.? Fates were kind, there were no fires whilst they were away.

Some of the fires in those days were trivial affairs. When the brigade was called to a fire in Chapel Street on the 2nd April, 1899, they put it out with a few buckets of water. Sometimes there was greater tragedy. On the 9th May a fire occurred in a bedroom on the first floor in Chapel Row. The damage was £20—quite an amount for those days. The report stated that the owners were not insured. Another fire in Mill Lane was attributed to boys playing with matches and setting fire to bedding. At Clayhall a shed and a small van were totally destroyed by fire on 22nd May and a poor donkey in the shed was burnt to death.

It was on Christmas Night 1899 that Mrs. Windsor's Boot Shop in the High Street caught fire. The fire started in the kitchen and was caused by a lighted candle being placed too near a rush basket. The brigade put out the fire with some difficulty. A little before that at the "Crown Tap" a nasty fire which took some two hours to extinguish broke out in a bedroom where a baby was sleeping and spread to an adjoining room where there were three other children. The four were got out just in time to avoid loss of life. The Superintendent pointed out that had these fires occurred at a distance from the station they might have proved disastrous. They showed the need for much more up-to-date fire fighting appliances than the old manual pump.

The need was reinforced in July 1900 when a very serious fire broke out at Mr. Crossland's furniture stores at 10.50 p.m. The brigade was there within seven minutes. The manual fire engine was set in action but it took four hours hard work before the blaze was under control. What caused great difficulty was the interference of the sightseers. Equipment was damaged and one fireman was injured as he was dislodged from a wall through the hauling of the hose by the crowd. But so grave was the danger that the fire brigades of the service establishments were called on for help. The lesson had been learned. Promptly the Committee accepted a tender for a new 300 gallon steam fire engine with necessary accessories at a cost of £449. A new era had dawned and with it greater responsibilities and greater costs. A new steam fire engine involved a competent man to take charge and so Mr. Mortimore was reappointed as Superintendent of the Fire Brigade not at £5 a year, but at £80 a year with free quarters.

Another source of argument and controversy was the continued existence of the Gosport Fair held on the Green near the harbour.

The two annual Fairs continued to be held on 4th May and 10th October on Gosport Green close by the Harbour. The Bishops of Winchester continued as proprietors of the Market and its Tolls for 600 years. The eighteenth-century Market Hall was a wooden Hall carried on timber piers, with two small rooms in which the Lord of the Manor held his courts. The Market was held underneath the building. These old premises were destroyed in 1802.

Meanwhile there were demands in the growing town for an Assembly Hall of reasonable size. The first proposal was to organise a lottery with shares of £25 each the proceeds after meeting the prize money, to be devoted to the new Hall. This new scheme did not prove successful. Then in 1811 a group of people got together and after negotiations with the Bishop of Winchester for the purchase of his rights over the Tolls of the Market, secured an Act of Parliament enabling them to erect a new Market House on the foreshore. The Act of 1811, which was amended by a further Act in 1828 gave the Trustees of the Market House very wide powers, which embraced not only the Market but the bi-annual Fair as well. By these Acts they obtained special powers over two pieces of waste land, upon part of which they built such things "as are usually sold in fairs" within the town of Gosport and, further, the sole right of Keeping and holding two Fairs annually, one on the 4th May, the other on the 10th October and of collecting the rent for any stalls. The Market House was a large building, square in shape, with white brick facing. Below there were warehouses, and on the main floor a large Court House. The Market was held, not within the premises, but on the land immediately adjacent. The Acts were passed with the approval of the Bishop of Winchester whose ancient rights were bought out.

For many years after 1812 the Market House on the beach was the main Market centre and Court House of Gosport. Later on the Main Hall was used as a Drill Hall for training volunteers. But towards the end of the Century there were frequent and bitter complaints about the Hall itself, the Market and the Fair. The Hall was considered unsuitable as a place of assembly and by 1884 it was replaced by the Thorngate Hall. The traders with shops in the town complained vigorously against the stall holders in the Market who came into the town, undercut prices and frequently sold contaminated food. There were particular complaints about the sale of doubtful fish. But the greatest and most violent objection came from many of the townsfolk about the Fairs held in October and May. The roundabouts, swings, fat ladies and peep-shows all evoked strong protests. It was claimed that the young people were corrupted by the lurid sights of the Fair ground and that the sober citizens of Clarence Square, hard by, were kept awake by the din.

Once the new Thorngate Hall became available the agitation to sweep away the old Market and the Fairs grew considerably and by 1896 the new Urban District Council began to demand its abolition. On the 12th March, 1896, a public petition from a large number of local inhabitants was submitted complaining that the Fair was a nuisance. The Council acted cautiously. It instructed the Clerk to find out who were the owners of the Fair, how they came by their rights, what the rights were, for what sum the owners would be prepared to give them up, what was the annual income from the stall holders in the Fair, by what right and by whom a levy was made on market gardeners and others coming into the town and over what area the Fair was permitted to extend?

Some members were not satisfied with the answers that the Trustees had considerable rights under the Acts of 1811 and 1828 and that the Council would have to purchase these before the Market and Fair could be abolished. When the Fair was held on 4th May, 1896, there were demands to know why the Surveyor and his assistants were seen employed in constructing a booth and who was responsible for cleaning up the mess after the Fair had ended. The surveyor replied that he and his assistant were not employed in erecting a booth but in pulling one down which had been set up in the roadway. A further report indicated that it would not be possible to do away with the Fair or Market without compensating the trustees who were unwilling to disclose the amount of revenue derived from Tolls or to state the sum for which they were prepared to surrender their rights.

So the argument went on. The Trustees denied that they were collecting Tolls from any market gardener who came into the town, although they had a right to do so. Every time the Fair was held the complaints from the residents in the vicinity became more vociferous and the demand for its abolition more blatant. Finally, however, a way out of the difficulties was found, and for £100 the market rights were bought out and extinguished.

Some other people in the town were urging that the newly established Urban District Council ought to consider the provision of houses for workers following the passing of the Housing of the Working Class Act 1890.

But the first attempt to interest the local authority in housing was not so successful. From 1870 the idea that local authorities might themselves build and manage housing estates in their areas received wide publicity. It was regarded as one of the ways in which reasonable premises might be provided in replacement of some of the worst slums. In 1890 an Act of Parliament, called the Housing of the

Working Classes Act, gave wide powers to local authorities to control housing conditions, but by Part III of the Act those authorities which decided to adopt the scheme could themselves build and manage estates. This was the real beginning of municipal housing, and some local authorities, including Leicester, Merthyr Tydfil, Liverpool, and Southampton prepared housing schemes. By 1896 when Gosport and Alverstoke had become an Urban District Council some local inhabitants began to agitate for houses to be erected by the Council so that some of the more dilapidated slums of the highly congested area around the harbour, with their dreadful conditions of sanitation, could be replaced. They decided to proceed by way of a petition to the local authority calling on them to adopt Part III of the Act of 1890 and local inhabitants were invited to sign.

Already it was becoming clear that the congested rows of tenement dwellings with their narrow courtyards which made the old town picturesque but highly insanitary would in time disappear and ever since 1851 there had been a movement out of the centre and towards the newer areas bordering Stoke Road and Forton Road. The population was increasing quite quickly but not within the area around the harbour. In 1851 the total population of the whole town was 16,353. It was estimated that there were then 3,168 houses in the whole area of Gosport and Alverstoke of which 1,628 were within the ramparts of the original town. How densely packed were those dwellings can be seen from the fact that 750 houses existed in 104 courts and alleyways in the town. The average rateable value of all the houses in the town area was only £6 10s. 0d. per annum. By 1896 conditions were improving slowly. The total population had increased to 26,000 and the number of houses to 5,700. But within the central part of the town itself the number of houses had declined from 1,628 to 1,300. The picture in 1896 was that the total number of houses was increasing by about 100 a year but entirely in the outlying areas. Within Gosport itself the removal of the worst of the old courtyards and alleyways was leading to slightly improved conditions of housing. But many factors were encouraging workers in the Dockyard to seek housing accommodation on the Gosport side. Rents were lower, property more available in Gosport and recently great improvement had been made in crossing the harbour by cheap steam launches which could land workers near to the Dockyard Gates. All these were inducements to come over to Gosport to live.

In consequence many people were urging that the newly formed Gosport and Alverstoke Urban District Council should itself undertake the duties available under Part III of the 1890 Act and build its own houses for the working class. Signatures were collected and finally when 500 names had been secured a petition was submitted by

Dr. Kyffin to the Council at their meeting on the 8th October, 1896. It was referred to the General Purposes Committee for a full enquiry. In December, 1896, the Committee submitted its report. It called attention to the rapid growth of the area as a whole, but the gradual removal of the worst slums in the town area. It stated that approximately 100 houses per year were being erected most of them much better from the structural sanitary aspect than those that were being replaced, but it acknowledged that there was still a large need for the five and six roomed houses. In 1891 the model clauses of the Local Government Board with regard to house sanitary conditions had been adopted and had been applied as far as possible in order to prevent new houses being substandard. The Committee recognised too that the Urban District Council was in the very favourable position of being able to borrow money for 35 years at 3¼% to embark upon housing projects. But they concluded their report in a negative way. "Your Committee have yet to learn that the position has arrived at an acute stage". "Your Committee cannot help thinking that Gosport and Alverstoke is a district where private enterprise and private capital can and ought to supply the need". Their final recommendation was, "Your Committee while in no way wishing to veto due discussion and perhaps ultimate consideration with a view to the adoption of Part III of the Act, at the present cannot recommend your District Council to embark on a venture so large and so important, until it is conclusively shewn that the objects of the memorialists are not to be attained by private enterprise".

There was a long argument about the report. Some members thought that insufficient evidence had been produced as to what other authorities were doing in the matter and called for further reports.

The matter came up again in February, 1897, when there was again a very full and involved discussion. This time there were demands that the Medical Officer of Health be required to report on any area or place he considered to be in an unhealthy or insanitary condition. It was realised that if serious outbursts of infectious diseases were to be avoided the Public Health Acts would have to be more rigidly enforced throughout the District. But having taken that step the Council decided that houses of the kind they would recommend for erection under the Housing of the Working Classes Act could not be built and let at the rent contemplated by the petitioners, i.e. 4/6 to 5/- a week. They then passed the following rather extraordinary resolution, "That Part III of the Housing of the Working Classes Act 1890 be adopted but in view of the fact that during the present year a number of houses for the working classes will be erected by private enterprise, no action be taken at present for putting into force its provisions".

Mr. Hart, a prominent member of the Council, was furious with this decision and promptly declared that he would move at the next meeting "that there should be erected in a prominent position a block of Model Lodging Houses, similar in character to those in Glasgow and London and also to improve an important thoroughfare in this town" (the area involved being the lower end of North Street). But the project was never proceeded with. It took the havoc and ruin of two major wars, the devastation and fury of Hitler's bombs before the model flats in the older part of the town could be constructed on the wastes of once congested courts and alleyways.

Perhaps the most interesting of the discussions of the period was the proposal, made before the establishment of the new Urban District Council, that Gosport should become a Borough.

The question of the organisation of local government was much in the air during the early 1890 period. The government of the day proposed a new measure which came into force in 1894 and which created the Urban and Rural District Councils as well as the Parish Councils.

The agitation going on at the time made some of the local Councillors, fully conscious of the growing importance of the town and discontented with the status of an urban sanitary authority, begin to think in terms of becoming dignified as a borough. There were in Hampshire at the time quite a number of small towns, such as Romsey, Andover, Basingstoke, which had acquired Borough status by ancient charter and throughout the ages had boasted their Mayor, Corporation, Aldermen, Councillors, Civic Mace and Estates. When the Municipal Corporations had been reorganised in 1835 and 1882 these towns, much smaller than Gosport, nevertheless retained their civic status and rights. Gosport was merely an urban sanitary authority with no charter (at least none that anyone could discover) and in local government it had no real existence before 1851. Some people thought it wasn't good enough—whatever the place was called—that it should be merely a sanitary authority or even an urban district council, and not a borough. An urban district savoured too much of the "lower-deck" whereas a borough gave dignity, civic pride and status.

It was on Thursday the 13th July, 1893, even in the days of the Local Board, that the issue was raised at the monthly Council meeting. It had been a busy meeting. Members were furious with the Water Company which they alleged was failing to maintain a reasonable supply; they were delighted to hear of a considerable improvement in the railway service and decided to print, at their own expense, copies of the new time-table; they were requested to approve the new-fangled telephone as a way of reporting fires, and they promptly deferred the matter—some members considering the telephone to be far too revolutionary an instrument. They considered a possible site for a new isolation hospital at Ham Lane, Elson, and they approved the annual salary of the Medical Officer of Health at £80 (and incidentally referred back a suggestion for an increase). Having completed all this business the following notice of motion was submitted.

"That the clerk be instructed to prepare a return showing the probable cost which would be incurred in obtaining a Charter of Incorporation for Gosport and Alverstoke and to obtain such information as would guide the Board in the event of its being considered desirable to take the necessary steps to procure the same".

As can well be imagined there was a long and acrimonious debate. Nearly every member took part, views and counter-views were expressed and charges and countercharges were made. Some members argued that dignity and status went hand-in-hand, others that added dignity would mean additional expense and up would go the rates. The mover of the resolution pointed out that it merely called for information and didn't commit anyone. Finally a vote was taken—ten were in favour and six against.

A few months later—on the 12th October, 1893, to be precise—the Clerk submitted his report to the Council. He indicated that under the Municipal Corporations Act of 1882 it would be necessary for a petition to be sent to H.M. the Queen (Queen Victoria) through Privy Council. He outlined the long, cumbersome and tedious procedure (which has changed very little to this day) for the acquisition of Borough status. On the question of local support he pointed out that a poll of the inhabitants might have to be taken. The minimum cost would be about £250, but if there were local oposition the costs might be doubled or trebled. The Clerk referred to recent applications made at Torquay and Bournemouth where there had been objections and it had been deemed necessary to engage Counsel at high fees.

The complicated procedure and the probable high cost frightened off many of the members. It was decided to thank the Clerk for his report and leave it at that. This was the end of the first attempt to make Gosport a Borough. The issue was not raised again until 1905 when it was defeated at a public meeting said to be one of the most rowdy ever held in the town. It was not until 9th November, 1922, that Gosport became a Borough with a Mayor and Corporation.

CHAPTER 17

Draining a Growing Town

As we have seen, in September, 1896, after a series of attacks by the Admiralty and War Office, the Drainage Committee appointed a firm of consulting engineers to prepare a general scheme of drainage for the area. But it wasn't until August 1898 that the proposals of the consultants (Messrs. Law and Son) became available. There was an immediate outcry of indignation. The estimated cost of the scheme was £50,000 which to the poor ratepayers of Gosport seemed an impossible amount. But, secondly, there came a shattering threat from H.M. Treasury that since there had been undue delay about the whole matter they would not assent to any increase in the contribution to the district rates arising from the new scheme of valuation recently introduced. Further, if the issue was not settled within a reasonable time they would consider suspending all further payments (amounting to about £6,600 a year) in lieu of local rates. The Admiralty delivered a knockout blow by declaring that they were not willing to make a grant towards the cost of the new scheme.

After three special Council meetings and a visit to Exeter to examine the new septic tank system adopted in that town, revised plans were produced by the consultants and these were finally submitted to the Council and approved. But by this time the estimated cost of the project had risen from £50,000 to £76,756—indeed some said to £89,000. This would involve a burden on the rates of £4,000 a year, equivalent to a rate of 8d. in the pound.

It was in these circumstances that a public meeting of ratepayers was called on Wednesday evening, 2nd June 1900, at the Thorngate Hall. It was a crowded, wild and angry meeting. There was bitter opposition to any drainage scheme at all, passionate attacks on the government, and furious objection to the cost of the project. The Chairman reported to an awestruck audience that the government already owed £690 in respect of unpaid increased grant and might well go on a rate strike. It had no legal obligation to make payments in lieu of rates and it might well adopt the attitude "no drains, no rates". The Chairman of the Council said he knew it was unpopular but he didn't think the provision of drains would bring financial ruin. People would not come

127

to a town that was not drained. In a speech lasting an hour and forty minutes he moved a resolution urging the people of Gosport to accept the main drainage scheme prepared by Messrs. Law.

He sat down and the meeting was at once in an uproar. His eloquence was unavailing, his arguments ridiculed and his pleas rejected. It was by now nearly 10.00 p.m. and the audience was becoming impatient. Complaints were made that the speeches were too long and a time limit was imposed. There was intense opposition. Some one moved, amid prolonged applause, "that the ratepayers view with alarm Mr. Law's scheme of drainage for Gosport and Alverstoke on the ground of its likelihood to entail a cost equal to the entire rateable value of the parish and decline to give the scheme any sanction until more definite information can be obtained as to the initial aid to be rendered by the government authorities both in regard to capital grant and maintenance contribution as originally promised; the ratepayers also protest against the form of coercion exercised by the Treasury in withholding part of the contributions previously agreed upon in aid of the rates". It was a shocking thing, like an octopus sucking at the very vitals of finance. The rates were already 1/8 a half year in the £—this would involve another 1/-. Another speaker who claimed that the citizens were in favour of some type of main drainage, was shouted down.

But it was Mr. Groom who voiced the strongest opposition. "Why should the liberties of Englishmen be taken away in this reckless fashion and why, whether they liked it or not, were they to have a thing (a main drainage scheme) shoved down their throats". "How were they going to pay the enormous sum mentioned? It was going to lead to universal bankruptcy and were they going to see their houses and children robbed? What caused the smells in Gosport was the dead cats floating in the moats. There was nothing to complain of but that. The extra 8d. rate would not do at all, they would find themselves in shoals tramping over to the Official receiver". The applause was wildly enthusiastic—the ratepayers cheered excitedly.

The amendment was carried overwhelmingly on a show of hands. It was late, very late, well after 11.00 p.m., and the weary citizens streamed out of the Thorngate Hall to sleep restlessly on a hot summer's night dreaming of sewage pipes, cesspits, dead cats in the moat, a government on a rate strike, higher rates, visits to drains in Exeter and septic tanks draining into the Solent. This was the beginning of the 20th century in Gosport.

This stormy protest meeting on the night of the 2nd June, 1900, when the residents of Gosport rejected outright (against the advice of their councillors) the proposed drainage scheme for the district and hurled defiance at the bureaucrats of Whitehall, had immediate and devastating repercussions.

During July, 1900, two letters were delivered at the local Council Offices—both were official, O.H.M.S., both were ominous. The first, dated 13th July and addressed to the Clerk of the District Council, was from the Admiralty. "My Lords", it said, "are of the opinion that in view of the refusal of the ratepayers to endorse the action of the Council and proceed with the scheme (of sanitation) without further delay, Treasury contributions in lieu of Rates ought no longer to be paid". The second, addressed to the Chairman of the Council and dated 30th July, said that it appeared to the Lords Commissioners of the Treasury that the new drainage scheme would not be proceeded with and "in these circumstances My Lords have directed that no contribution in lieu of Rates shall be paid to the Urban District Council".

Calamity upon calamity. Dictatorship from Whitehall. Civil Service tyranny. The 20th century bombshell. The contribution instead of rates amounted in Gosport to £6,600 a year and without that grant the rates, already having reached the staggering and dizzy figure of 1/8d. in the £ and likely to soar immediately to 1/10d., would be nearly doubled. In awestruck tones the ratepayers bemoaned their lot. Either they must incur an expenditure of £80,000 for a drainage system with all the financial implications or they must endure a monstrous rate because the Government would not contribute. Was there ever such a dilemma? Have the drains and pay the price, or refuse the drains and forego the Government contributions. Some said the Government was merely trying to intimidate the ratepayers, others declared that certain councillors were behind it all and welcomed the threats from Whitehall as a means of getting their own way locally. The total budget for the whole year was about £12,500 and to contemplate a loss in revenue of over £6,000—to some it was just unbelievable. But facts were facts, and the directive had been issued; no local drains, no Government money.

It might be midsummer and the season of holiday-making but here was an emergency that demanded immediate action. The Roads and Works and Drainage Committee met at once. They saw the red light, the writing on the wall and they called a full meeting of the Council for Tuesday the 21st August, 1900. This was the resolution they submitted to the bewildered councillors: "That seeing the serious position in which the District will be placed by the withholding of the Government contribution and also that nothing can be gained by further delay, your Committee recommend that your Council do adopt Messrs. Law and Son's scheme and take the necessary steps to put same into execution according to the plans prepared by them and approved by your Council and that application be made to the Local

Government Board for permission to borrow the sum of £81,153 for carrying out the work".

Some described it as capitulation, some said the Council would be going down with colours flying, other declared it was inevitable. When the Council met to discuss the problem at 6.00 p.m. on that August evening there were still a few who wanted to continue the resistance. An amendment was moved that would have made the application for loan sanction subject to "having first sought and obtained the approval of the Ratepayers in Public Meeting assembled". This was an invitation to another meeting like that of the 2nd June. Wiser counsels however prevailed, only five voted for the amendment and sixteen against. Finally the resolution to proceed with the scheme and to apply for permission to borrow £81,153 was agreed to, sixteen voting in favour, four against and one sitting pretty. And so in September, 1900, the Council was able to make a rate of 1/10d. in the £, excessively high in the opinion of the ratepayers but certainly not involving the calamitous increase which the lack of government aid might have caused.

The Government, having won its victory, was not prepared to let the matter rest. Even while the Council officials were preparing the necessary documents, another broadside was fired. This time it took the form of a letter from the Local Government Board complaining bitterly about the disposal of the town refuse and the unsatisfactory condition of the moats. The Council was by now in penitent mood and ordered that a reply be sent to the effect "the greater precautions are being taken so that the refuse shall be deposited on land as far from dwelling houses as possible and that a portion of the refuse, where practicable, is being burnt". They added, "and as regard the unsatisfactory condition of the moats, this is mostly caused by the military authorities but will no doubt be greatly remedied when the proposed scheme of drainage is carried into effect.

By February, 1901, the negotiations for the new drainage system had reached an advanced stage and on the 11th February a public enquiry was held at the Council Offices into the application to borrow the money to proceed with the scheme. This was a far more decorous meeting. The War Office and the Admiralty were represented, most of the Councillors were present and about 22 of the representatives of the ratepayers. Explanations were given to the Inspector, but only few questions were asked by members of the general public. Everyone took the attitude that the sooner the whole sorry business was cleared up, the better.

Perhaps to the modern historian the most significant decision about the new drainage scheme was that the outfall was to be directed to The Solent and, in particular, to Stokes Bay. It was on the 15th June, 1901, that the Admiralty finally agreed the terms upon which the drainage outfall would be allowed at Stokes Bay.

By November of 1901 all the plans had been prepared, tenders invited and the Council met in solemn conclave on the 8th to hear the worst as to what the cost would be. To their relief the lowest tender was £77,260—somewhat lower than had been anticipated. Even that wasn't the end. The contractor refused to sign the documents and it wasn't until the 6th March, 1902, that the matter was finally settled, at the same cost with another contractor.

Did the Government relent? What happened about the contributions in lieu of rates? It wasn't until May, 1902, that the Chairman of the Council was able to report the receipt of a letter from the Treasury stating that they would pay the sum of £2,000 in satisfaction of the arrears of contributions. The negotiations had been delicate and at times it seemed unlikely that the Council would get back the amounts that had been withheld. It was with a sense of relief that the following resolution was passed: "That the very best thanks be accorded to Mr. Cooke for his service in connection with recovery from the Treasury the sum of £2,000, part of arrears of the government contributions". It was carried unanimously.

And so the work of providing a satisfactory drainage scheme with its outfall to the Solent commenced. It was in any case a formidable undertaking, involving the construction of some 26 miles of sewers at a rate of about 2 miles a month. Few people, however, who were connected with the struggle which had gone on for nearly 25 years, to provide a sewerage scheme adequate for the area, realised that within another 25 years the population would have doubled and that by 1960 there would be serious doubts as to the adequacy of the system to modern requirements.

CHAPTER 18

The Early Years of the Twentieth Century

To people living at the time, the 1st February, 1901, must have seemed like the passing of an epoch. Not only had a new century recently dawned, but on that day the Royal Yacht bore the body of Queen Victoria, who for 64 years had symbolised the wealth, the majesty and the eccentricity of the British people, across the Solent and Spithead, through lines of draped warships firing minute guns and with flags solemnly at half-mast, to the shore at Gosport. On that day of grey misty wintry sunshine the Royal Yacht brought the coffin to Clarence Yard to be placed reverently on the Royal Train which steamed slowly through Gosport, past St. Matthew's School where so many times the Queen had watched local children at play, past the colonnaded elegance of Gosport Station and on past Brockhurst to Fareham and London.

It might well have seemed the end of an era. The twentieth century with its new scientific revolutions and its calamitous world wars was on the horizon. Locally there was evidence of the conflict between the old ways of life and the new forces of progress. The century had opened with a furious argument about the drainage of the town but in the end a modern system of drainage had to be adopted. The local council had also to buy out a disused public house for over £2,000, to remove its sign of the Dolphin and to transform the place with red paint into a fire station. An old gypsy encampment at Ewer Common was acquired to become the first public recreation ground. Another sign of the changing times was the building of the new premises designed to house both a free library and a technical college. The old fair held for centuries twice a year on The Green, which had become the object of bitter local attack as being the resort of tipsters and prize-fighters came to an end in 1901 when the Council bought out the rights for £100. Gosport was growing—the population had reached the 30,000 mark—the old ramparts with their thick walls, their moats, their huge arches and massive gates were gradually being removed and out to the west and north of the old town there were growing up new, although sometimes ugly estates of tenement houses. The narrow, rural, twisty lane leading out to Bury Arch and then on to Alverstoke and Stokes Bay became an urban thoroughfare. Still more remarkable the horse tram conveying passengers to Forton, Brockhurst and on to Fareham and the outside world, was by 1908 to become an electric tramway.

Education was changing its pattern too. In 1902, by the Education Act of that year, the Urban District Council became responsible for elementary education for some 5,000 children. Hitherto all the schools in the area had been provided by the churches. The Council took its duties seriously and between 1903 and 1913 three new public elementary schools were erected, the first in 1907 at Clarence Square on the site of the once famous Burney's Academy, the second in 1911 at Grove Road in the rapidly growing Hardway district and the third in 1913 at Stone Lane.

In this changing world of local affairs with the added responsibilities and enlarged functions, members of the local council began to see the opportunities of enhanced prestige. It was in 1905 that they announced that they considered that the town ought to have the dignified status of a borough with a mayor and aldermen and had resolved to petition the King in Parliament for the grant of a Charter of Incorporation. This decision set alight the most furious and bitter conflict that had raged in Gosport for many a year. It was argued that there would be the most tremendous increase in rates to meet the cost of civic pageantry, that there would be no improvement in local services and that, above all, it was calculated to submerge once again the interests of the folk of Alverstoke to the traders of Gosport.

The leader of the opposition was the redoubtable Admiral E. Field, who was M.P. for South Sussex from 1885 to 1900 and who, on retiring from the navy had settled in Grove House, Spring Gardens. Field was a tough, robust, bonny fighter with a gift for invective and the voice of a foghorn. He was determined to maintain the rights and interests of Alverstoke. He had bitterly opposed and resented the change in the name of the authority which had been made in 1892 and was violent in his antagonism to new-fangled proposals to take over the water company, the tramways, the electricity service and the dreadful scheme to embark on municipal housing. But the idea of a Borough of Gosport filled him with horror and rage. When in February, 1905, the Council resolved to apply for a charter Admiral Field made a violent, if characteristic onslaught. He regarded it as a case of the unruly, undisciplined, unkempt, unlettered child Gosport attempting to smother its stately mother Alverstoke. Admiral Field raged from his local quarterdeck. He called upon the people of Alverstoke to stamp on the proposal of the Council as they would stamp on a cobra. The ridiculous scheme was, he thundered, only advanced in order to gratify the lust for power, the arrogance and presumption, the urge for self-glorification of some Gosport individuals.

The statutory Towns Meeting was held at the Thorngate Hall in May 1905. It had been preceded by a torrent of threats, abuse and denunciation in the press and at meetings. It turned out to be one of the most remarkable demonstrations in the history of Gosport. The hall itself was crowded with angry ratepayers come to bait and deride their councillors. Those who couldn't get in crowded round the doors and climbed twenty feet on to the window ledges to let out a flood of angry, abusive and highly indecorous comments. The councillors hadn't much of a chance to argue the case against the jeers, cat-calls and threats. There was a tirade of yells that the councillors were lining their pockets, that Alverstoke was being ignored and that the costs both of obtaining borough status and also of maintaining its dignity would ruin the townsfolk. Amid cheers and boos the proposal was overwhelmingly defeated.

Not for another decade was the issue seriously raised again. Certainly not during the lifetime of the belligerent Admiral. The man who stormed round Gosport on a hard-tyred tricycle, who dominated the bench of justices, who kept two emus in his garden, whose booming voice struck terror into the hearts of colleagues and servants alike, lived on until March, 1912. It was ironic and characteristic that in his will he should have left his estate for purchase by the Council at a nominal price and it was typical that the offer should have been turned down by a Towns Meeting.

Then came war in 1914 and all thoughts of Borough status were put aside. But by 1918 when ideas of reconstruction were abroad it was decided to appoint an Incorporation Committee. It had a long, wearisome task. The local records are full of minutes of public inquiries, of the collection, sorting and appraisal of evidence, of submissions by Counsel and of interviews with high officials. All through 1919, 1920 and 1921 the prolonged business went on. But this time there was no Admiral Field to lead the opposition and details were gradually elaborated and objections surmounted.

Finally on the 17th October, 1922, the Minute Book of the Gosport and Alverstoke Urban District Council was closed with the customary vote of thanks to the Chairman, Mr. J. F. Lee, and on the 9th November at 12 noon precisely the first quarterly meeting of the Council of the Borough of Gosport was opened and it was resolved "that Mr. (within half an hour to become an Alderman) J. F. Lee, J.P., be elected Mayor of the newly constituted Borough". Yet there was to be caution in all things and no extravagance for while at the first meeting a Committee was appointed to consider the question of providing a Chain and Badge of office for the Mayor, at the next meeting the members defeated by a large majority a motion "That the time has come when the necessary steps to uphold the dignity of the Borough of Gosport should be taken and a Committee appointed to deal with the question of proper robes for the Mayor, Aldermen and Councillors and a suitable uniform for the Macebearer". The time hadn't come. The town was prepared to accept a Mayor and to provide him with a Chain but it would not tolerate a lot of dressed-up councillors parading their powers and revelling in their dignity.

At Christmas, 1901, the people of Gosport were eagerly awaiting the completion and opening of a new Technical Institute opposite the Town Hall. The project had aroused great enthusiasm. It was intended to give much needed new premises to the free public library as well as to provide a centre for the development of scientific and art education.

For some years there had been negotiations and at last in November, 1897, the local Technical Institute and Public Libraries Committee began a serious search for a suitable site. The preference was for an open space adjacent to St. Matthew's Square, but the War Department raised objections. Finally an alternative was proposed on a site from which the old ramparts were to be removed, at the junction of High Street and Walpole Road. The ancient archway had been pulled down and after a good deal of argument during which the District Council agreed to make a new roadway from High Street to North Street, the site was acquired for a sum of £800. Even to the members of the Council who in May, 1898, accepted this agreement because they were anxious to see the new technical institute erected, this seemed a princely sum to pay.

Preliminary estimates suggested that the new technical institute-cum-public library would cost about £6,000 to build. In November, 1898, the Technical Education Committee of the Hampshire County Council adopted the following resolution: "That on receiving notice from the Gosport District Council that the sanction of the Local Government Board to the purchase of the site has been obtained and on receiving from the Gosport District Council an undertaking under seal that a sum of not less than £4,000 shall be expended in the erection of a building and fittings on this site in accordance with the Building Regulations of the Technical Education Committee, then, that a sum of £1,000 be advanced to the District Council on account of the allocated grant of £2,000".

The Gosport District Council by adopting the Technical Instruction Act of 1889 could itself levy a rate of ½d. in the £, as a Technical Education Rate, but in 1900 that meant only £203 17s. 10d. for the year.

By Christmas 1898 the Council took possession of the site and started to clear the old ramparts and level the area. So keen were some

136

of the members that they instructed the Surveyor to proceed with the work of levelling the ramparts in connection with the site for the Technical College and to take on any additional labour he might think necessary. Since 5 pence per hour was the current rate for labourers—with loss of time for bad weather—the cost doesn't seem high by our reckoning. But in fairness it must be said that the Council had just approved the principle of a standard weekly rate for labourers—irrespective of weather. It was 19/- a week.

The Council decided to invite schemes by an architectural competition and asked H. H. Stratham, F.R.I.B.A. to act as assessor. He selected the design of Mr. Cross of Messrs. Spalding and Cross, a London firm of architects. So delighted were the Committee with the plans that they arranged for them to be on public exhibition in the Council Chambers for three days.

By March, 1900, the Council was ready to proceed. Tenders were invited. But when they were received there was a shock. The lowest tender was £6,693, much more than the Committee had anticipated. And it came from an outside firm. The Committee determined to knock off £600 and passed a pious resolution that the "savings" would not "impair, the area, efficiency and leading architectural feature of the scheme". The architect thought differently so did the Local Government Board and eventually some items were restored. One member argued fiercely that the lowest local tender (some £57 more than the lowest) should be accepted, but he was squashed. In August, 1900, the work of building began.

The next problem was to work out with the County Authority a plan for the control and administration of the new technical institute. Two special meetings of the District Council were held on the 18th and 22nd July, 1901, when it was finally resolved to adopt the scheme for the control and government of—note the title—"The Gosport and Alverstoke Science and Art Technical and Secondary School". Those responsible intended a comprehensive title. The first 6 members of the new governing body were nominated. They were responsible to the District Council.

Meanwhile work was in progress and the new improving edifice began to take shape. A search was made for a worthy dignitary to perform the official opening ceremony. The choice fell on Lord Northbrook and on Wednesday, 25th September, 1901, the new "Gosport and Alverstoke Technical Institute and Free Public Library" was officially opened. The enterprise of the District Council was applauded, the County Council representatives promised their help in the development of technical education in Gosport, then a town of 25,000.

The wonderful day passed. The remaining members of the

137

governing body—including the local artist Martin Snape—were nominated. The first headmaster was appointed—at a salary of £100 a year. The Clerk to the Governors got £20 a year and the caretaker 13/4d. a week. For the first month the total salary and wages bill, headmaster, teachers, instructors, clerk, caretaker was £39 8s. 8d.

It was a Wednesday, 15th January 1902, that the first pupils came to the new school. There were 32 of them (at least 31, since one started his career by being absent). In May, 1902, the number had increased to 40. Several scholarships were offered. The Henry Cort Memorial Trust gave the remainder of their funds, the Thorngate Trust awarded 4 entrance scholarships of £5 each. George Churcher gave 3 of £5 each.

But alas, the attempt to establish a Technical College in Gosport was in vain. During 1902 a new Education Act was passed which centred the functions of Higher Education in the County Council. Gosport lost its premises (apart from the section allocated to the library)—the County Authority entered into full occupation—although assisted by a group of governors appointed locally. The whole character of the school was changed from the technical school intended by the District Council to a grammar school—and so it remained until increasing pressure of numbers made it essential to erect the new Gosport Grammar School at Bay House, Stokes Bay.

Just off the new road into Gosport on the northern side is all that remains of Clarence Square, once the aristocratic home of Admirals, and the site of Burney's Academy, in its heyday the most famous of all naval training schools. There is still a substantial building in bright red brick, now part of a clothing factory, which was originally Clarence Square Boys' School, the first school to be built by the Gosport Urban District Council when it became a local education authority in 1903.

The school opened its doors on the 28th May, 1907, at 9.00 a.m. when 343 boys were on the roll. The premises had been built for 330, three rooms of 60 pupils and three rooms of 50, with a central hall. The headmaster was W. W. A. Colbran, and after a week in the school he wrote "For the first week the work has been most satisfactory and the behaviour of the scholars excellent. The acoustic properties of the school are all that could be wished and the arrangement of classrooms, lobbies, playground, offices are such that work can be carried out under the best conditions. The ventilation is splendid. The attendance this week has been exceptionally good". Fifty years later, regarded as substandard, the area around having been denuded of population, the premises were sold as a factory.

But in 1907 nothing of its ultimate fate was known. On the 20th June the school was officially named the Gosport and Alverstoke Clarence Square School No. 11, and was placed on the government grant list. The member of Parliament, Mr. Arthur Lee, presented a flag staff and on the 1st July the flag was publicly unfolded at 4.00 p.m. The children were formed up on three sides of a square in front of the main entrance. They first sang "Now pray we for our Country" and "Rule Britannia". Then the Chairman of the Education Committee spoke on the meaning of the flag and the growth and greatness of our world wide Empire. The flag was then unfurled, the scholars singing "God Save the King".

Those were spacious days, 80 years ago. But of course they had their other side. A fully trained certificated master in full charge of 60 boys was paid a salary of £85 a year increasing by annual increments of £5 to a maximum of £125, while a fully trained certificated woman teacher received £76 rising by £3 a year to £100. A supplementary teacher at the school, in charge of a class of 50 was paid £50 a year, a pound a boy a year. No wonder the rates were 2/3d in the £, and in the opinion of most ratepayers, ruinously high.

If special facilities were required in those days appeals had to be made to friends and parents. An appeal for help towards school prizes, for games material for the field and playground and for instruments for the school band produced the princely sum of £9.

But although the school started off in grand style, very soon the anxieties and perplexities of school life began to show themselves. On September 3rd the headmaster noted that 6 new scholars had been admitted to Standard 1 and that made the roll over 70. The attendance was not quite as good as it ought to be complained the head "40 boys are away this afternoon". Then there was Edward B . . . who on the 16th September was again sent home because of his verminous condition. "This boy has been sent home during the last three months a very large number of times. It seems useless to warn his relatives as they almost invariably dispute the fact although both the head teacher as well as the class teacher have seen this vermin again and again upon him". And of course there were troubles with the building. On October 10th the Chairman of the managers was called in to see the effect of heavy rains upon the roof and the playground. Accidents happened then as now. "The head teacher regrets to report that at 10.30 when the 1st class was lining up for drill in the play ground a boy named Annells collided with another boy, slipped on the ground and broke his arm. The Head Teacher at once went for medical assistance and had the arm set and put in splints".

On the 29th October the school acquired a new Museum Case and the Headmaster reported a week later that the school museum had been put in order. "A number of interesting curios have been sent up from the boys' parents and from friends of the scholars so that the museum now contains a variety of articles some from distant parts of the world, such as China, which will prove very useful in teaching geography etc.".

There is a popular belief nowadays that children in school are not so well taught as they were in the good old days and that in particular the "3 R's" have suffered. How many parents and employers complain that their young people cannot spell or write, or do arithmetic in the way they could in the older days when there was better discipline and more concentration on basic subjects. It is somewhat refreshing to find the Headmaster of the new school writing on the 11th December 1907—at that time, when the boys came to the school for the first time "the results were extremely disappointing, many boys being hopeless in spelling and little better in mental arithmetic—two most important subjects". And even after the first six months work in the School he says "The boys, however, are very weak in spelling and written arithmetic, weak in reading and a portion of them weak in discipline". And of another class he writes "Reading in common with most other classes is weak, as is also spelling and arithmetic". Even a year later, in December, 1908, the Headmaster reported "Standard 1 has greatly improved in spelling but in a written test of arithmetic previously prepared they have done extremely ill, the greater part of the scholars not getting a simple sum right out of five set".

There were important events in the life of a schoolboy in the years before the first world war broke out in August, 1914. The records tell that on the 8th May, 1910, the Head Teacher addressed the scholars on the "startlingly sudden and momentous news of the death of His late Gracious Majesty King Edward VII", but by the 10th May, "This day was kept in Gosport as the one set apart to officially proclaim the accession of His Majesty George V. Morning school was held as usual but just before noon the senior scholars, some 150 in number, were taken to the steps of the Thorngate Hall from whence the Chairman of the District Council, T. McCully, J.P., made the proclamation. A very large gathering of troops, the general public and school children were present. In honour of the unique occasion Mr. McCully announced a half holiday".

In November, 1911, the Head Teacher noted that the weather had been very bad during the last week or two. "Many of the scholars, owing to their bad foot gear, have repeatedly got wet footed. The Chairman of the Education Committee called last week and inspected some 20 or 30 boys whose boots were in a very unsatisfactory condition. He is considering the best plan for meeting the difficulty without pauperising the children. A boot club has been suggested in which the main part of the money could be raised by the contributions of the children themselves. Several children who have their feet coming through their boots and whose stockings are equally as bad have come to school lately soaking wet". On December 15th we read "a dozen or more children have been selected for boots".

The Clarence Square School made a notable contribution to the fighting forces during the first World War. One of the most impressive occasions in its history was on the 17th April, 1920, when a memorial to 109 old boys who died during the war of 1914–18 was unveiled. In an eloquent speech the Headmaster said "Since 1788 there has been a school on this site, and perhaps the most famous was Burney's Academy where men, trained for the Navy, had gone forth and worthily upheld the traditions of the British Empire". The then Commander-in-Chief Admiral Sir Cecil Burney had written, "I treasure the pleasanter memories of my boyhood at the old school in Clarence Square and I know how well pleased my masters of those far off days would have been to know that the school which has followed there on the same site has so gallantly upheld the traditions of its predecessors".

Recently, when the new Grange School was being built at Rowner, considerable difficulty was experienced with laying out the playing field because it was discovered that a concrete runway of the airfield traversed the area. This is a reminder that Gosport was not only a main air station during the two world wars but that much of the early history of aviation in this country is centred in Gosport.

It was in October, 1909 that the Portsmouth Aero Club started to use a site of about twelve acres alongside Fort Monckton for experiments in gliding and flying. But the next Spring, in April 1910, the club moved its headquarters to Grange field and from that time many of the first experiments in heavier than air machines were conducted. The great genius and the financial power behind the work was Patrick Alexander. He displayed temendous zeal as well as great courage in pioneering the early aeroplane and most of his personal fortune was devoted to the work. He settled on the Grange field in a caravan and gathered about him a band of enthusiasts who built gliders which could travel for about a quarter of a mile reaching a height of some 50 feet. Every Saturday when the weather was reasonable, and sometimes when it wasn't, Alexander gathered together his cronies for what seemed a useless sport. But to him it was a matter of serious importance.

The club started on the 9th April, 1910, with demonstrations of gliding by Alexander, but quickly other machines were built. Many of these were flimsy affairs and some ended disastrously. One of the first gliders was built by two officers at Fort Blockhouse and dragged up the harbour but collapsed on its attempt to fly to Grange. Another, even more interesting was constructed in a yard in Elmhurst Road, Gosport by two naval lieutenants, Stocks and Cochrane, but this also crashed when the first attempt to fly it was made at Grange. But from these reverses Alexander and his colleagues learned a great deal. For the next few years many experiments in powered aircraft took place at Grange. One of the very earliest of the pioneers, Lieutenant J. C.

Porte, an officer in the submarine service learned to fly abroad and in 1913 brought the first aircraft, a Deperdussin, to land on the Grange airfield. The plane had a mechanical fault and a Mr. V. Hutfield who was keenly interested in motor engineering, and whose garage was at the corner of Harding and Brockhurst Roads, helped with the repairs. One of the very early machines which had in fact flown for a few hundred yards before crashing was stored and later exhibited at his garage.

In 1912 the Royal Flying Corps was established and the Grange Airfield became the home of one of the seven squadrons forming the Military Wing. It was in January, 1914, that the Royal Flying Corps took over Fort Grange and the airfield as a headquarters. This was only about six months before the outbreak of the First World War. Once the war started the military squadron went overseas but within a few months arrangements were made to use the airfield to train a Naval Aeroplane Squadron and from that time there were tremendous developments. Under Commander Longmore the whole area around became the most important centre in the south for aircraft training. Fort Rowner was taken over and what had previously been a polo field, a race track and a training site for the military now became one vast airfield. These early aircraft were soon put to good service to attack the huge Zeppelins sent over by the Germans to raid the southern cities.

In 1917 the Gosport School of Special Flying was established at Grange. This was largely the result of the remarkable developments in the techniques of air fighting which had come about as a result of experience over the Western Front where many of the pilots had been killed and their aeroplanes destroyed through lack of thorough training.

During the course of the first world war tremendous technical improvements were made in the production and efficiency of aeroplanes, as, of course, was the same in the second world war. By 1917 the aeroplane which had been the play toy of the wealthy and the dream of the adventurous, became a major instrument of war. Slight and crude as they were by modern standards they were rapidly becoming a vital factor in military strength. The main problem by 1917 was not so much the production of planes as the training of the crews, both pilots and observers. It was quickly evident that mere enthusiasm and daredevilry which excited young men to take up flying was not enough. The emphasis had to be on highly trained efficiency.

It was at the Gosport air station that both the need for intensive training and the means by which it could be achieved were first worked out. The method was to recruit a body of instructors who were themselves provided with a detailed code of training principles. When

142

the Air Council was established early in 1918 it used as a basis for the new schools of flying throughout the country the programme of instruction worked out and operated in Gosport. It was very largely because of the extraordinary standards of efficiency in training which were adopted in the years between the wars, when resources were seriously limited and government interest in the service was at a low ebb that the small but highly proficient Royal Air Force was able in 1940–41 to withstand the German onslaught and to expand at a rapid rate while at the same time maintaining its tremendously high standard. So distinguished was the contribution made at the Grange Station at Gosport, through which most of the highly ranking officers passed at one time or another, that one of the series of the Avro 504 planes was named the Avro Gosport in honour of the place the station occupied in the growth of the R.A.F.

Throughout the period from 1918 to 1946 Gosport Air Station remained a major centre for training pilots and other air crew and it attracted a cadre of highly skilled and qualified specialist officers who made the study of aeronautics their life interest. But it was becoming obvious that the station was unsuited to the requirements of modern aircraft, and soon after the war ended in 1945 it passed over to the Royal Navy first as a helicopter centre and later as an engineering training school. The last link with the world of flying came in 1955 when the Ministry of Supply's Aircraft Torpedo Development Unit at Gosport closed down.

At the Gosport School of Special Flying the first concentration was on highly skilled instructors following a carefully devised programme of training. Machines which could simulate every type of problem to be met in flying were evolved, the dual control plane was developed and a special means of communication in the air between pilot and crew, trainer and trainee, known as the Gosport tube was installed. It is particularly interesting that the Royal Naval Aircraft Repair Yard (Fleetlands) has adopted some of the exacting standards which were used in the Gosport School of Flying. Fleetlands is one of the most highly efficient undertakings in the country with a remarkably good and effective training scheme for apprentices. During recent years it has made a noteworthy contribution to the study of management at a level far above that of most commercial undertakings.

17.   Haslar Hospital with Forbes Bridge. Note the watermen plying their trade.

18. Camper and Nicholsons and Ratsey and Lapthorn's buildings with 'Victory' moored offshore.

MARTIN SNAPE. WATERCOLOUR C 1910. PRIVATE COLLECTION.

19. Watermen conveying passengers between Portsmouth and Gosport. Note the Market House prominent in the centre of the picture. Early nineteenth century.

ARTIST UNKNOWN. GOSPORT MUSEUM COLLECTION.

20. Burney's Academy, Clarence Square. Early nineteenth century.

21.　Winter scene at Coldharbour.

MARTIN SNAPE. WATERCOLOUR C. 1906. PRIVATE COLLECTION.

IRON FOUNDRY AT GOSPORT.

ARTIST UNKNOWN. GOSPORT MUSEUM COLLECTION.

22. Iron Foundry at Gosport.

23.   The Green, Gosport, showing some of the old eighteenth century houses typical of the town area.

MARTIN SNAPE, WATERCOLOUR C 1905. GOSPORT MUSEUM COLLECTION.

24. Flagship saluting, showing the Market House in the left background. Engraving, early nineteenth century.

25.   The India Arms Hotel, 1959.

26. One of the original eighteenth century houses in Clarence Square. C 1959.

27.   Fine eighteenth century house in the former Portland Terrace, the site now occupied by the four storey blocks of flats in South Street. C. 1959.

28. Coldharbour, St. Matthews Square with part of Clarence Square in the right background.

MARTIN SNAPE. WATERCOLOUR C 1906. PRIVATE COLLECTION.

29. Gosport landing stage.

MARTIN SNAPE. WATERCOLOUR C 1910. PRIVATE COLLECTION.

30. View of Portsmouth Harbour from the shore near Burney's Academy, pupils of the Academy in the foreground.

LITHOGRAPH. C 1840. PRIVATE COLLECTION.

C 1910 PORTSMOUTH CITY MUSEUM

31. Stoke Road, Gosport.

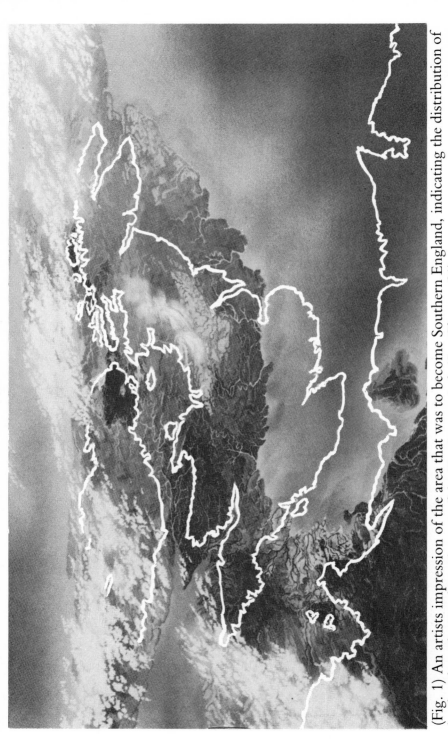

(Fig. 1) An artists impression of the area that was to become Southern England, indicating the distribution of land and sea during the early part of the Tertiary period. (See Chapter 21).

CHAPTER 19

Gosport during the Years between 1918 and 1945

The war years 1914–1918 were times of feverish activity and occasionally of desperate anxiety in Gosport. Its alleyways resounded to the hilarity and the quarrels of conscripted seamen on leave. For a few years foreboding prosperity paraded itself. There was the youth, gaiety and the mocking of war time triumphs and the sombre reality of destruction, for when a naval vessel was lost countless families in Gosport were shattered with bereavement. The Battle of Jutland in 1916 resulted in the deaths of 6,000 men most of them from the Portsmouth and Gosport area. For a time there was tempestuous excitement, high wages in the Dockyard establishments and a frantic fight with death at Haslar Hospital.

Just before the 1918 war the population of the town was about 33,000. At the census in 1931 it had reached 37,928, an increase of about 5,000 in twenty years. Most of the new families came in towards the end of the period. After the war had ended in 1918, and for another decade the place relapsed into its local life of outward dullness and vigorous internal controversy. The town's war memorial, a new hospital, was commenced in July, 1921, when Field Marshal Earl Haig laid the foundation stone and was completed in April, 1923. The Royal Marine Light Infantry whose barracks were at St. Vincent contributed largely to the scheme. No sooner was the hospital, which was also the official war memorial of the Red Marines, completed than the Red and Blue Marines were merged and took over the barracks at Eastney, leaving St. Vincent empty for some four years.

To the outside observer, especially to one coming across the harbour and walking up the High Street, Gosport seemed stagnant. Brian Vesey Fitzgerald probably took only a cursory glance at the ramshackle High Street and the crowded delapidated alleyways and courtyards and didn't much like what he saw. He described it in his book on Hampshire. "Over an arm of the harbour, reached by ferry, lies Gosport, which although a separate town is so much a part of Portsmouth in fact and tradition that it must be dealt with in the same breath". This was no compliment, for he was not fond of Portsmouth either. Gosport, he described as the storehouse of the navy.

"Everything the navy needs is stored in the Victualling Yard. The shore seeps round from Nicholson's Yard to Blockhouse Point and then over a bridge (which is incidentally still a toll bridge) to old Haslar Hospital which is still the Navy's Hospital and was built in the 18th century. It is, for a hospital, quite a handsome building and it is entered through a pair of very handsome gates. But, for the rest, Gosport is far from attractive. A vast quantity of the houses are old but they are also poor and mean and shabby. The place has a melancholy look, like a man dying slowly from an incurable but not painful disease. Somebody renovated the church and ruined it in doing so, but fortunately left the timber arcades which are simply wonderful and a feature worth going a long way, even worth a trip on the crowded ferry, to see. And Gosport has one other claim to fame. Somewhere in the town Henry Cort of Lancaster set up his forge for iron puddling. In 1740 which was the year in which he was born, Britain produced only 48,000 tons of pig iron. Little more than a century later we were producing more than eight million tons and that was due entirely to the experiments and the genius of Henry Cort. Yet Cort, as is so often the case with men of genius, died poor and broken hearted. Some one else got the money and the honours. All he got, and that so long after he died that he would not worry about it anyway, was a panel over the entrance to Gosport Public Library—and the tale is told that there was a real squabble over that since most of the people most concerned had never heard of him and did not believe that he had done anything wonderful and that if he had, he had not done in in Gosport".

But appearances are deceptive, especially to the casual viewer. Had Brian Vesey Fitzgerald gone into Nicholson's Yard he would have seen some of the greatest craftsmen at yacht building in the world yielding the adze with the precision and skill of masters. The most famous racing craft, the Shamrock IV and Shamrock V and the Endeavour I and II were the products of technique and craftsmanship long departed. To have walked through Quay Lane, narrow and decrepit as it may have seemed, was to be on the hallowed ground of designers and workmen whose standards were exacting and whose products were impeccable. At the other end of Quay Lane were the sail lofts of the greatest sail makers in the world, Ratsey and Lapthorn. Surrender to steam they might, but reduce quality they never would. The dignity and bearing of these workers, their confidence in their skill, their pride in their craftsmanship were an indication that behind the seeming decay of old buildings there was vigorous life. For a foreign potentate to possess a yacht designed by Nicholson and built to the fastidious standards of the Camper Nicholson Yard was an ambition even greater than to own a Rolls Royce. The skill was passed on from generation to generation. Young boys at school were brilliant at carving model craft and it was a high achievement to be accepted as an apprentice at Nicholson's Yard.

Nor were the Naval depots as dull as Vesey Fitzgerald might have thought from external appearance. For at Fort Blockhouse there was being established the submarine basis of the Navy. Nearby H.M.S. Hornet was the centre for the naval coastal craft which were to become the famous M.T.Bs. (motor torpedo boats) of the 1939–45 war. With their skill in training, their risky experiments, their exacting standards of discipline and their devotion to duty in a period of apathy and economy, the men of these craft toiled on, and, in the event, stood between the country and invasion. Indeed, as we have seen, some of the problems and principles of air strategy were being worked out in the hangers at Gosport Air Station. A more spectacular aspect was occasionally to be seen. For a time Stokes Bay, facing the Solent and Spithead, became the focus of the impeccable drive for mastery of speed in the air. Thousands from Gosport and elsewhere celebrated on the beaches at Stokes Bay on 10th September, 1929, when Flying Officers Waghorn and Atcherley flew the Supermarine 56 at 330 miles an hour to break the world's speed record and win the Schneider Trophy.

Haslar hospital, although still reached by a toll bridge, had its occasional excitements. Haslar had always lived apart from Gosport. But it gave employment to many people living in the neighbourhood. During the latter part of the 19th century Haslar was the scene of fierce internal conflict between the naval administrators who knew little or nothing of medicine and the trained naval medical doctors. Discipline was strict and yet difficult to enforce because a large number of naval pensioners had taken up residence at the hospital; indeed quite a number of civilians managed to get residence permits. They brought their worldly possessions, including sometimes their pet parrots, and settled in for life. A legend was told of an aged pensioner who demanded 1d. from the clerks at the Hospital to pay the cost of the return fare by ferry across the harbour. The rigid disciplinary code denied him this so he walked round the harbour, some thirteen miles via Fareham only to collapse and die when he reached Porsmouth. More certain is the scandal of the burials at Haslar. Originally the area adjacent to the hospital was used indiscriminately and anyone digging in the land around might well come across bodies buried without coffins in shallow soil. So serious did the matter become that the parish burial ground next to Alverstoke Church was used for a time. In 1859 the new naval cemetery at Clayhall was taken into use. The walk across the grounds within the Hospital to get to Clayhall was known as the "Dead Man's Mile". In 1881 the first Royal Naval Medical School was founded at Haslar but only after 1900 did it become an essential part of the establishment.

Delightful anecdotes about life at Haslar during the first World War are given by Halliday Sutherland in "The Arches of the Years". He tells how he reached Haslar at noon. "Haslar is separated from Gosport by a creek crossed by a bridge. In the creek is also a jetty opposite the hospital gates. To go from Portsmouth to Haslar you cross the harbour, here half a mile wide, by public ferry to Gosport, or more quickly by naval transport to the hospital jetty. At Haslar I was conducted by a senior officer to report to the Surgeon-Admiral. On entering his room I took off my cap but my companion said "Keep it on. You're on the quarter deck". I was puzzled as to why the floor was called the quarter deck and presently discovered that the entire hospital was named in this fashion. My bedroom was 'a cabin' and my bed a 'a bunk'.

Halliday Sutherland goes on to describe how he got up at 7.00 a.m. one Christmas morning, walked to the Gosport jetty to get the eight o'clock ferry for Portsmouth only to discover that it was not running that morning. The only craft alongside was the beautiful white steam pinnace flying the White Ensign belonging to the Commander-in-Chief from whom he begged a passage for an outing to Brighton which was strictly forbidden. When he returned that night at eleven o'clock on the Portsmouth jetty he found that there was no ferry to Gosport. The gates of Haslar would be closed at midnight. He contrived to get the dockyard police to summon help. "Within fifteen minutes a large tug with steam up was alongside the quay. I was the only passenger and on the short voyage stood on the deck looking at my watch. The tug came alongside the Haslar jetty. There was no time to thank her skipper because I had to sprint for the lodge gates. These I reached and as I passed the great clock of Haslar began to strike the hour of midnight".

Many residents of Gosport have wondered whether they were in time for the last ferry and what conveyance there would be on the Gosport side. The journey round the harbour—"going round the Victory" as it used to be called—is still a journey to be avoided if possible—at least to those without the ubiquitous motorcar.

In part the dingy appearance of Gosport during the years between the wars was due to real poverty. Dockyard pay was low, employment difficult to get and whilst employment in the Dockyard might be secure it involved accepting a relatively low standard of living. Gosport was not affected by the tumultuos events of 1926 when the General Strike occurred but there were large numbers of unemployed as the naval service was run down in successive economy drives. Life was hard and the town took on a look of poverty. There were alternate cries for schemes of work for the relief of unemployment and demands for a rigid economy. The early enthusiasm for working class houses, which had led to tenders being accepted for 430 Council houses by April 1920, died down when it was found how costly these could be and how slow to erect. By May, 1921, only 12 had been completed. Other schemes seemed more rewarding. The old "cockle-pond" at Walpole Park near the Haslar Creek was converted into a model yacht pool and became a centre for national events in the model yacht racing world. A nearby site which for centuries had been the open space of the walled town was transformed into a large open air swimming pool. Much more was expected from this lido than was ever obtained. Of greater immediate value was the construction of a new wharf, a floating pontoon and gangway which improved communications with Portsmouth, but cost the ratepayers £59,983. Schemes were prepared for the transformation of Stokes Bay into a seaside resort but the only part of the scheme to materialise was a public lavatory.

The hard times had an effect, too, upon education development. Competition for apprenticeships in the Dockyard was severe and an extremely high standard, especially in mathematics, was called for. Once in the service, the training was rigorous, the opportunities few, but the security much greater than outside. The Dockyard School afforded opportunities for clever boys to become craftsmen of a high order. In Portsmouth a number of private schools existed where the whole purpose of the curriculum and teaching was to obtain places in the extremely competitive dockyard examinations. In Gosport the Borough Council determined to establish a school for selected boys who would prepare for "dockyard entrance". The Central School in Gordon Road was opened in 1927 and from the first it aimed at a very high standard of attainment in Mathematics and English and quickly achieved a remarkable reputation for the successes of its pupils in entrance to the Dockyard. A few years later, in 1932, a school for girls was established. These selective central schools became an important feature in the education pattern of the town, but such were the dictates of economy that the premises consisted of the essential classrooms only, with no hall, no library, no gymnasium—and these were never added.

Although there was an atmosphere of poverty about the old town area, where many properties were falling into decay and the picturesque 18th century alleys rents and courts were becoming slums, the rapid growth of the new housing estates in the Brockhurst and Elson area, which attracted a large number of residents from Portsmouth, meant that the building trades were reasonably prosperous. Money was to be made on these new estates and one local resident who found that the demand for houses involved a demand for wallpaper, for light tools, for shops, for cinemas, quickly establised a fortune. The wallpaper factory in Lees Lane provided much needed local employment, particularly for women.

Rapid growth brought its problems. Before the war of 1914–18 there had been much criticism of the water supply in the town which had remained under the control of a private company. The records of the Urban District Council are full of complaints. There were protests, deputations, exhortations, demands that the Council should buy out the company which had been established by Act of Parliament in 1858. The waterworks at Bury Cross, which relied upon deep wells, had become inadequate to the needs of the growing town. Additional works were built at Foxbury at the northern end of Portsmouth Harbour. In 1902 there were allegations that supplies from the Foxbury wells were contaminated with sea water seeping through the chalk from Fareham Creek. There was a bitter controversy and rival reports from analysts were bandied about. In the event the Council found itself unable to buy over the water company. A new site was acquired at Soberton some eleven miles from the town where deep wells were constructed. It was not until 1937 that new powers were obtained to ensure an adequate supply.

Similar problems arose in the case of electricity. The original supply was provided by the Provincial Tramway Company from their works at Hoeford. The old horse-drawn tramway service which had been started in 1870 finally became an electric tramway service in 1908. But bitter complaints were made about the inefficiency of the supply and the delays in the installation of the service. One doctor complained that the lives of his patients were in constant jeopardy from the alarming practice of cutting off the electricity supply at midnight, while the Council protested that houses were wired for electric light for two years before the supply was connected. In her account of Holy Trinity Church Mrs. Barclay tells how at the beginning of 1914 electric lighting was installed in the church and she adds—the Vicar wrote in the Parish Magazine these words "The new installation was first used on January 18th. It meant the total disappearance of gas from the church, including, we trust, the pervading scent of that illuminant. What chiefly pleased at the outset was the softness and unexpected warmth of the light, the ease with which it could be manipulated either to light up the Church or to throw an unoffending congregation into total darkness. On the second Sunday, a message for 'More Light' procured the extinction of all we had plus the lamp outside the Churchyard".

After the conferment of Borough Status, Gosport began to expand rapidly both internally and externally. Early development had been in the Forton and Newtown areas where some dockyard workers settled. Some of these came from Portsmouth to take advantage of the cheap rents on the Gosport side. It was after the first world war, and particularly after 1930 and in the Brockhurst and Elson area, that the trickle from the other side of the harbour became a flood. The Council was forced to develop housing schemes, it even appointed a Housing Manager, but in Brockhurst, Elson, Hardway and Ann's Hill large new private enterprise estates began to emerge. A comparison of the Ordnance Survey maps for 1898, 1912 and 1939 shows the extent of the provision of new housing accommodation in the north-east part of the town.

The lack of land for housing development, near enough to the Dockyard which was a feature of Portsmouth's civic life between the wars, and which led a number of people to take up residence in Gosport, began, after the town had become a borough, to affect Gosport as well. There is inevitably a land problem in a town with a water frontage on three sides. But in Gosport the Ministry of Defence owns a huge part of the 6,000 acres. While the Borough would be happy to have some of this land made available for residential and civic purposes it would not wish to be deprived of establishments that afford employment to its citizens or brings in a substantial contribution to its finances.

So the only way of expansion had been to the north and at the expense of Fareham. It is not surprising that within a few years of acquiring Borough status, Gosport added Lee-on-the-Solent and Rowner to its area. The name Lee-on-the-Solent, as it is correctly written, is of modern origin. It dates from 1884 when Mr. C. E. Newton Robinson who was in a yacht in the area was so impressed with the prospects of Lee that he urged his father, Sir J. C. Robinson, to buy the foreshore with the idea of developing a new health resort.

Although Lee-on-the-Solent had all the advantages of a newly planned community it was too early to benefit from the experience of Welwyn, Letchworth or Hampstead and over the grand design came the patchiness of individul construction. Lee has in more recent years become a favourite residential centre. Although Lee-on-the-Solent is recent, the name Lee in various forms, meaning a clearing in a forest area, is a common one. In 1236 it is recorded as being held as a manor by Gilbert de Brut. In this period it was written as "lige" or "ly" or "le". So we get Lee Britten (or Lee Brittain). There is a delightful old world cottage of the Elizabethan period in Lee but in 1839 only three houses are shown in the area and its transformation into a seaside, residential district came only after 1910.

With Lee-on-the-Solent came the wonderful foreshore stretching from the Browndown Ranges to Hillhead and Southampton Water. It was a coast liable to erosion and ultimately would involve the Council in heavy coast maintenance but its aspect across the Solent to Cowes and Lymington was one of great attractiveness. The narrow twisty military road which cuts across Browndown from Lee to Stokes Bay and thence via Privett and Bury to Stoke Road provides the only direct link between Lee and Gosport and meant that although it was constitutionally part of the Borough it formed an isolated and independent unit. A light gauge railway led from Brockhurst to Lee but was never a successful venture.

By the time the second world war erupted Gosport presented the apparently conflicting pictures of a dull, sleepy, decaying town with few attractive features, and at the same time a vigorous thriving and expanding community. The population which had increased only slowly from 33,301 in 1911 to 37,928 in 1931 had reached 45,910 by 1938 and over 50,000 by 1939. The birth rate was extremely high, the town was expanding rapidly in area, huge new estates were being built and some of the older slums were being replaced. A new era in the life of Gosport was emerging.

War interrupted, but did not halt, the expansion of Gosport. In the event it hastened it. Derelict and decayed buildings, over the demolition of which there would have been interminable disputes and delays, were destroyed at a blow. Bombs settled arguments about the replacement of slums. Gosport immediately became, and throughout the war remained, a front line town, at first vulnerable to attack and then a spring board for counter-attack. Whilst bombing added to the superficial drabness of the appearance of the town, the twenty service establishments within its boundaries became scenes of intense activity. Supplies from Priddy's hard and Clarence Yard, ammunition from Bedenham, submarines at Ford Blockhouse, motor torpedo boats from Hornet, the fleet air arm from Daedalus all were a vital part of the war effort. Into Gosport came vast numbers of seasoned naval officers and untrained recruits. Houses and schools were commandeered to become residential quarters or training establishments.

With the first nervous impact of war Gosport was declared an evacuation area and mothers and children of school age and under were invited to seek safety in the rural parts of Hampshire. Nearly half the 6,000 schoolchildren in the town were marshalled in special trains at the historic Gosport station and evacuated to Droxford, West Meon and elsewhere. The authorities stepped into the vacated schools to turn them into first aid centres, rest centres, training units and even office accommodation. Two new schools due to open officially in September 1939 were immediately requisitioned.

Soon schooling restarted, teachers visited homes, schools not otherwise occupied were opened for an hour or so a day, while shelters were built in playgrounds. At first a trickle and then large numbers of evacuated families began to return from the safer rural but less homely areas. Gosport was home and for the first few months of the war the threatened devastation did not take place. Gas masks, black-out, shelters, fire watching, rationing, identity cards, ferries which stopped soon after dusk, uniforms, the nervous tension of a war without local incident strained the nerves of the inhabitants.

"The 'phoney war' came abruptly to an end. The little harbour craft were called on for the Dunkirk operation. Bury Hall at Alverstoke became the headquarters of the newly formed Home Guard." The talk of invasion became a serious threat. Gosport was dramatically in the front line. The bombing of the town started in August 1940 when the area around the Town hall was damaged. Feverishly, underground shelters were completed while nearly every garden had its Anderson shelter. The winter of 1940 was a time of trial. Night after night as darkness fell, the wail of sirens sent people to shelters. Incendiary bombs gutted the old Market House, the Thorngate hall, the new Ritz Cinema, the old Theatre, the Dock House on the waterfront. Twisted burned out beams gave the town a sombre appearance. But the worst ordeal came during the early months of 1941 and particularly on the nights of 10th January and the 10th March when major raids were made on the harbour area. After the fierce onslaught of the 10th January (the night when the Guildhall of Portsmouth was gutted with fire) there were no public services in the town for some days—water and gas mains were destroyed and not for a week was normal life restored. Most nights during that dreadful period bombs shattered homes and shops, and the town began to take on a battered look. The worst attack of all came on the night of 10th March when serious damage was done throughout the town. More than half of the houses in Gosport were affected by war damage. Although many people lost all their possessions, casualties were fortunately few.

During the latter part of 1943 the town began to acquire a new outlook. Gradually the harbour and Stokes Bay were transformed into embarkation beaches for the assault on Normandy. Tension mounted. Gangs of Irish labourers turned Stokes Bay into a mighty concrete platform, the sections of the Mulberry harbour began to be assembled, and the streets echoed to the rumble of tanks being brought to the landing craft. A week before "D" day came the last air raid on Gosport when bombs were dropped near the Holy Trinity Church killing four people and destroying an infants school. The following day the school was re-established in two rooms at the Clarence Square Boys' School. The pupils had been rehearsing for a May Day festival. From the rubble of their school they dug out the ruined clothes and the next day presented before the Mayor the crowning of the May Queen. Peace came in May, 1945, and with it the task of reconstruction.

CHAPTER 20

Post-War Gosport and future prospects

In the company of so many towns and cities at the end of the war, Gosport saw a large increase in its population. The rise was in part due to ex-servicemen returning to their families and to the phenomenally high birth-rate which would later have a dramatic effect upon the school building programme.

In 1931, the census figures showed Gosport's population at 37,298. Twenty years later, there were 58,279, with a forecast of further growth. Housing, as a consequence, was given top priority by the post-war Council. While relatively few people had been killed by enemy bombing—111 civilians, consisting of 48 men, 42 women and 21 children—over 10,000 incendiary bombs and over 600 high-explosive bombs had been dropped on the borough. The bulk of this deadly weaponry fell in and around the town centre area. It is not difficult to understand why this was—the High Street is ringed with large military establishments that assumed even greater significance in wartime. They were satellites to the huge and vulnerable Dockyard across the Harbour, and all were prime targets. By the end of the war, Clarence Square, one of the town's best claims to architectural distinction, was a sad ruin. Holy Trinity Church miraculously escaped the attention of the bombers but not so the picturesque (albeit overcrowded) houses and cottages that huddled close to it.

This wholesale destruction of town properties had been foreseen by the local authority and as early as 1942 plans for the reconstruction of a post-war Gosport were under consideration. In the same year, the Planning Committee produced a new road scheme for the town centre, taking the traffic out of High Street through South Street and allowing for the widening and re-development of Coldharbour. The predictable shortage of post-war housing was catered for by a proposal to purchase all land within the ramparts for municipal housing. In retrospect, this was a bold scheme which, had it been implemented, would have reinforced the town centre as the focal point of the Borough. It would also have ensured the eventual restoration of both Clarence Square and South Street. But the plan—imaginative as it undoubtedly was—became subject to delays due to the necessity for compulsory purchase orders to be taken out, and to the settlement of claims arising out of war damage. It was further correctly deduced that the huge estimate of desperately needed housing accommodation could never be satisfied within the limited confines of the ramparted, old town.

So it was that the High Street environs were deliberately left derelict in favour of a huge new development on the outer edges of the Borough. The War department was persuaded to surrender 64 acres of land, including the ancient parish of Rowner with its little hamlet of Bridgmary, to the Council for what was destined to become a major experiment in modern municipal housing. The creation of the Bridgemary Estate, as it was first known, was quite properly hailed as one of the most remarkable post-war housing developments anywhere in Britain. For several years Gosport was the nation's leading authority in housing, due largely to the foresight of one man, Alderman Bob Nobes, Housing Manager and Gosport's Mayor from 1946 to 1949. The Navy made its own contribution to the scheme with some 200 homes comprising the Victory Housing Estate. By the late 1950s the original Bridgemary Estate had grown into a community with a population approaching 20,000. It is a fact that municipal housing far outstripped private enterprise ventures until the early 1960s.

The inroads upon open spaces were such that by 1962 it was becoming more and more difficult to find additional land for housing. The land problems of Gosport were made more serious by the insistence of the Service authorities in clinging to wide areas. Crown lands in 1949 covered more than half of the 6,215 acres in the Borough. After intense local pressure some small stretches of land were released but not on a scale sufficient to make any effective contribution to the problem.

Even worse was the determination by the County Council as Planning Authority to restrict, or at least delay, any further expansion of Gosport. The conflict between the Borough as Housing Authority and County Council as Planning Authority was only one facet of an antagonism which embittered relationships between the two during the years immediately after the war.

In 1948 the Hampshire County and Portsmouth City Councils invited Mr. Max Lock to prepare a comprehensive analysis on the future development of the city and South-East Hampshire. The Max Lock Report was duly published in 1949. It described Gosport as "a town handicapped by nature and by history. . . . The town is connected with Portsmouth by ferries and by devious land routes with the rest of England. It developed in the 18th century as part of Portsmouth Naval Base and soon acquired victualling yards, barracks and hospitals. During the 19th century this single function came to

155

dominate the life of the town. The broad belt of land stretching across the peninsula was added to by the other large areas already owned by the Crown. Employment by the Services grew until it now forms nearly half of the total of 11,000 insured workers.

"Although the town has made some headway in overcoming this lack of balance in function, it has never been able to overcome the effects of its isolation. Today its seaside resorts at Lee-on-the-Solent and Stokes Bay attract visitors from a limited area but its shopping, commercial and administrative centre serves only the town's needs. Some manufacturing industry has been attracted but it employs only some 10% of the town's workers. Its residential areas have some small pockets of blight, but their chief defect is the restricting and dividing effect of Crown land."

This very thorough report studied many new angles. It recommended that the population of Lee should be allowed to develop from 4,000 to upwards of 11,000 in order to re-house the overspill from Portsmouth. Fortunately for the peace of mind of Lee residents, Leigh Park took over this function instead. But in another area—the matter of access into the Borough from both Portsmouth and Fareham—the Lock Report sounded dire warnings with regard to the future that in retrospect should have been heeded then and there.

At the time of the report, the Gosport and Portsmouth Steam Launch Company was operating a 16-hour shuttle service from the pontoon at Portsmouth Harbour station to the landing stage at Gosport. It carried a daily average of 24,000 passengers. The report drew attention to the limited quayside accommodation and the need for buses to be brought to run alongside the ferry concourse which, it suggested, ought to be fully covered. "The huge cross movement of workers, shoppers, business people, service personnel and train passengers for London, reflects Gosport's close economic ties with Portsmouth," commented the report, which went on to note that while the ferry service was efficient, delays and inconveniences were caused by the distance between the bus stops and the ferry, particularly on the Portsmouth side.

At the time of the report, there still remained the floating bridge which crossed the Harbour on chains from Gosport to Broad Stret. Although antiquated in the extreme, somewhat unreliable in operation and capable of carrying only about twenty cars at a time, the floating bridge nevertheless provided an easy access between the two places for as many as 2,000 vehicles each week. But throughout the fifties, it became less economic and eventually ceased to function altogether.

The Max Lock Report recommended that a representative board should investigate the possibilities and potentialities of a tunnel linking Gosport with Portsmouth. Since most vehicular traffic was having to

156

enter the already congested West Street area of Fareham, the report stressed the very real need to create some other way in which motorists and tradesmen in vans and lorries might more easily travel between Gosport and Portsmouth. When the floating bridge finally came to an end, various committees and study groups on both sides of the Harbour came up with many suggestions. The practicability of providing a bridge, tunnel, a "Kearney" tube, a hovercraft service or a fixed vehicular ferry was examined. A joint committee of Gosport and Portsmouth authorities came to a conclusion that the only feasible solution was a fixed ferry which could link Coldharbour on the Gosport side with The Hard at Portsmouth. The cost of installing such a service was estimated to be £520,000 with annual running costs of £91,400. However, when it came to meeting the initial cost, Portsmouth was not interested and Gosport could not afford it.

"The increase in population on the Gosport-Fareham side of the harbour, the tremendous growth in the number of cars and other vehicles, the complete breakdown of all vehicular traffic across the harbour, the serious congestion of the A27 in Fareham, West Street, have all combined to make this problem one of pressing if not desperate urgency," wrote Dr. White in 1967. Twenty years later, despite all the money that has been spent on flyovers, round-abouts, junctions, alterations to the A32 and Newgate Lane, the problem of getting through Fareham remains extremely serious. Countless schemes of improvement have been proposed throughout the years. Some have been carried out, but each attempt at alleviation has been ultimately defeated by the inexorable increase in the volume of traffic.

A survey in the 1960s recommended the construction of an eastern by-pass crossing Hoeford Creek. In the 1970s, the idea of a Gosport-Fareham Link via Lee was put forward, and this proposal is still favoured—although since it is based partly on the existing Newgate Lane and Broom Way thoroughfares, it may become just another route to the same bottleneck. An alternative idea was the building of a new road to the east of the present A32—but the way is blocked by the ubiquitous land ownership of the Ministry of Defence. Recently, the idea of a light-rail transit system out of the borough was put forward, a scheme which enlightened towns and cities elsewhere have studied and experimented with in depth. Such a suggestion does at least provide alternative thinking to the blinkered perception that car driving is the only way to travel. Of course, had local people in the 1950s shown less apathy with regard to the town's transport problems, there might still be a passenger railway link with Fareham. Not only would a regular railway service go some way towards alleviating the rush-hour horrors, but also it would have opened up the possibility of a direct link to London, since Fareham may well be favoured with such a service once the local lines have been electrified.

But as it is, commuters by car must resign themselves to the dismal, daily crawl to and from the borough. Quite apart from the delays and dangers caused by the jams, there are other negative aspects for Gosport. It is difficult for the town to attract new industry and shops—despite cheaper rents than Fareham can offer—when access to Gosport is so difficult. Certainly the Council has recognised the need to bring in new job opportunities. Examples such as the transformation of the former Sandersons factory into a centre for small business, the re-development of the old George White factory site and the expansion of Sweetheart Plastics have been useful; but the general trend remains for people living in Gosport to work elsewhere.

Within the borough itself, some of the traffic problems that were increasing in the 1960s have been solved. In 1979 the building of the South Relief Road eventually reduced congestion in the approaches to the town centre, but only at the cost of the demolition of eighty homes. A year later, further improvements came about as a result of the opening of Haslar Bridge to vehicular traffic. Road safety was brought into sharp focus in 1987 when statistics showed that cyclists were at great risk in Gosport and various opinions were voiced concerning the road hazards in the town. Certainly many of the roads in the borough are somewhat inadequate for the present-day volume and size of vehicles; but it must also be added that driving standards have declined sadly over the years. There are constant complaints that drivers do not obey speed limits, that consideration and good manners on the road are largely absent, that aggression rules the day. The reckless speeding along the narrow confines of Cambridge Road and the selfish and illegal parking on the north side of the High Street in Lee are just two examples of the sad decline in standards. Another recent trend in 'traffic control'—the 'filtering-in' system as in operation at the junction of Foster Road and the South Relief Road—seems only to serve the principle of traffic flow at the expense of safety. Must such features sacrifice cyclists and careful, considerate drivers to the aggression of speed merchants and over-laden lorries?

For the time being at least, traffic has been banished from the town centre. Pedestrianisation is part of the scheme devised by the council to help the heart of the town, the High Street shopping area, to maintain a steady enough beat despite the proximity of Portsmouth and the Fareham precinct which have placed our town centre in a lower position in the shopping hierarchy. During the 1970s, people generally thought that shopping in Gosport was quite pleasant and easy to cope with—especially with free car parking—but compared with Fareham's comparative cornucopia of consumer goods the High Street was found

158

somewhat lacking. Shoppers complained that there was not enough choice in the shops, that there were not enough cafes or toilets. The fine new library, the improved ferry gardens with the bus station that had replaced the draughty old stands, contrasted alarmingly with the dismal remains of North and North Cross Streets. These roads, through an unfortunate combination of circumstances, had become a half-derelict area wherein, it was reported, were to be seen rats, wild cats and even snakes. By the late 1970s, there were a dozen empty shops in the town centre—well-known names such as Crown Paints and Lipton's had ceased to trade, along with smaller supermarkets such as Dee Discount and Shoppers' Paradise which were too small to combat the allure of newcomers to the fringe of the shopping areas, such as Asda and International.

Meanwhile the Council proposed to make improvements. Plans were made to pedestrianize the High Street and to promote it as a conservation area, and to develop a new shopping square at the northern end of North Cross Street. Despite powerful opposition from some traders, High Street was closed to traffic in 1988 in a six-month experiment. As we write, pedestrianization has been extended for a further period and some of the opposition to it has faded away. The novelty of an unpolluted, safe High Street seems to have the effect of relaxing shoppers, especially those with prams and push-chairs, and the chance is there for further development of retailing and related functions. At the same time, the strong sense of unity and community often shown by the shopkeepers and traders in Stoke Road has helped this interesting and varied alternative shopping centre to overcome the decline of the 1970s. It seems that the Council has been proved right to maintain the separate identities of Stoke Road and High Street, even though they are close together.

Another aspect of life which has come increasingly into focus over the last few years is the question of the use of leisure. Immediately after the war much of Gosport's social scene, as in pre-war days, was still centred around the cinema and the separate-sex organisations of men's clubs or Townswomen's Guilds and related groups. Until the 1960s there were four cinemas in the town—the Forum in Stoke Road, the Criterion in Forton Road, the Ritz in Walpole Road and the cinema in Lee Tower. This latter building was always a talking point, partly because it was, from the first, somewhat of a financial white elephant. Much was expected of it after the war, and it became at various times a restaurant, tearooms, ballroom, theatre and bowling alley; but sadly, neither private enterprise nor the local authority could make it a viable proposition and it eventually closed in 1970. The entire Tower complex was demolished in 1971. It can be argued that environmentally this was a disaster. The slender white Tower lent distinction, and exciting views, to an otherwise unremarkable seafront. By the 1980s buildings of the Tower's period were being listed—Southampton's Civic Centre is a case in point—and it is entirely possible that had the complex been less of a financial burden we should still have it with us today as a thriving and attractive amenity.

In the 1950s, the national mood for Community Centres had burgeoned in Gosport to the extent that a large and flourishing Centre was developed in Bury Road around the pleasing early nineteenth century, Bury House, with the handsome modern additions of the Thorngate Hall and a modern ball-room and theatre. Dr. White himself played a very large part in the adventurous community scheme. Eventually other Community Associations appeared, at Bridgemary, Elson and, after tremendous local efforts, Lee-on-the-Solent.

The town's sporting life was invigorated after the war, with strong football, rugby, cricket and other team games developing solid organisations. The Borough Football Club, formed in 1944 through the efforts of such men as Stan Cribb, Bill Adams, Jack Eales and Morrie Richardson to name just some, has developed through the local leagues to its present position of a successful member of the Southern Premier League, now known as the Beazer Homes League. Through its emphasis on team-spirit, loyalty and fair play, the Club has been a most successful ambassador for the town of Gosport.

As befits a maritime town, the sea has brought in sporting opportunities, particularly since the 1960s. Yachting and sailing—once the preserve of the upper-middle classes and captains of industry—became 'de rigeur' for all classes and ages. In the early 1960s, a proposal for a yachting marina at Stokes Bay drew both praise and criticism from all sectional interests within the Borough. The original scheme was for a 600–1000 berth marina covering 35 acres and cutting deep into the Gilkicker grasslands. The shoreline facilities were to include fourteen 3-storey residential blocks, hotels, restaurants and a ballroom. The idea was hotly debated in the Council chamber but eventually foundered, partly through hostile public opinion but mainly because the Ministry of Defence who own much of the land at Gilkicker refused to give way. Meanwhile, the environmental lobby was slowly gaining momentum and the public mood was for Stokes Bay, an area of outstanding natural beauty, to remain unspoilt by development. Local people did not want to rival Southsea or Brighton.

By the late 1950s, the town's remaining eighteenth and nineteenth-century buildings were mostly in urgent need of repair and restoration. Although a number of them were listed by the then Ministry of Housing and Local Government as being of historic and architectural worth, the prevailing Council mood was to go for demolition rather than rehabilitation. Gosport's philistine attitude towards its own architectural heritage earned the justified opprobium of both the Civic Trust and the Royal Commission of Ancient and Historic Monuments. The last-named body highlighted Gosport as one of the four towns in England that had destroyed a particularly large number of historic buildings, most of which had been capable of restoration and integration into the town's built environment. Even in retrospect it is hard to defend the local authority's attitude. The ensuing catalogue of destruction is depressing to read. Between 1961 and 1965 the bulldozers were very active. Among many others they demolished Clarence Square, a group of interesting old cottages in Chapel Row, the Hall on Trinity Green, the eighteenth-century navigation column in Clayhall Road, the stone archway to Forton Prison in Lees Lane and several of Gosport's famous old public houses. Another depressing feature was a seemingly endless wrangle with British Railways as to whether they or the Council had responsibility for the fine old railway station, which meanwhile fell into dismal neglect. A sixteen-year-old schoolboy, Stephen Weeks, attempted to hold the demolition of the Hall by drawing attention to its plight with the Ministry of Housing and Local Government. Although he successfully 'spot-listed' the Hall, an administrative bungle delayed this information reaching the Council until the demolition men had done their worst. Many councillors remained unrepentant. In 1962, for example, Fort Brockhurst was described as a 'horrible monstrosity' because it was standing in the way of valuable development land.

By the time more enlightened approaches towards town planning began to surface, irreparable damage had been done. Nevertheless, one good thing at least emerged from the ruins of such civic despoliation— the development of Trinity Green. The decision to build 11 and 16 storey blocks of flats in this low-lying region was at first controversial and unpopular, but over the past two decades the bold scheme has come to be, if not loved at least admired as an arresting piece of townscape. For height, in this district of uniform flatness, is an asset in itself and from the flats the most breath-taking views of the Harbour and the Solent can be enjoyed. This, together with the clearing away of the alleyways and passages surrounding South Street opened up the vista of the Harbour and gave Gosport people a dramatic new seaboard entrance to their town. The treatment of this area altogether is a credit to the county and Borough authorities. Though the piles of rectangular concrete sometimes make one nostalgic for the narrow alleys, the shadowy pubs, the press gangs and smugglers about their nefarious ways, the grandeur of far-off naval victories or the stark tragedies of shipwrecked sailors, in short the whole historical background to this area of the town has been lost.

By a strange irony, when, in 1975, the Council decided upon a policy of 'high-density infill' building on this site, public opinion was outraged. The press aptly labelled the ensuing fracas 'The Battle of Trinity Green' as councillors, residents, preservation societies and the Department of the Environment locked horns, the Ministry endorsed the 'no infill' campaign. At about this time, the North Street area was undergoing development and similar arguments focussed on the plight of several interesting old buildings which were under threat. The former home of James Biden the brewer, No. 6 Seahorse Street, was the subject of a public enquiry when the Department of the Environment stopped the Council's proposed demolition of this listed building. Since then, it has been successfully incorporated into the new development together with the cottages facing it.

Gosport ventured into Europe in 1959. In July of that year, cultural, sporting and civic links with the French seaside town of Royan were established. The twinning link with Royan was to flourish for the next two decades before arguments about funding began to threaten the happy relationship engendered between the towns. One of Gosport's best ambassadors in France and indeed elsewhere has been the Silver Band. In 1967 the idea for its formation was given impetus and encouragement by the then Minister for the Arts, Jennie Lee, and the Director of the Royal Marines School of Music, Colonel Vivian Dunn. The decision to have silver instruments was taken because cleaning them would be less difficult than the usual brass ones.

Education in Gosport has undergone many significant changes during the last few years, particularly at secondary level. Brune Park was opened during the 1960's as a bi-lateral 11-18 school, formed from the amalgamation of Walpole Road, Fisgard Road and Clarence Road schools. It was built on land which once belonged to the prominent Prideaux-Brune family—hence its name and badge. In 1975 another new school, St. Vincent, was created on the famous site which once housed marines and sailors. This exciting venture was Gosport's first 'Community School', for its 32-acre site also included a £200,000 activities centre whose facilities could be jointly enjoyed by both school and public. Meanwhile, with the education chiefs committed to comprehensive Education, the Grammar School became known as Bay House and merged with the former secondary modern school at Privett. During the late 1970s, however, the problem of falling school rolls began to emerge. It became clear that the four secondary schools—Bridgmary, Bay House, Brune Park and St. Vincent—could not each sustain a sixth-form.

Thus in 1977 Hampshire Education Committee proposed the setting up of a Sixth Form College to serve all 16-19 year-olds in the

162

borough. There were many plans, many arguments, and much opposition. Vigorous meetings to discuss the matter were held in various schools and eventually the then Education Minister, Mrs. Shirley Williams, rejected Hampshire's proposals.

But the inexorable decline in the numbers of sixth-formers carried on. By 1980, the Sixth Form College plan was being resurrected. This time most of the opposition faded away before the demographic inevitabilities. Finally in September 1987 the Gosport Sixth Form College opened on the St. Vincent site—the county's first Community College and a venture in which Gosport people can take great pride.

Upon the shoulders of many of the young people who are at Gosport's schools today will fall the mantle of carrying this town into the twenty-first century. Let us hope that they will continue our tradition of healthy and vigorous local pride which has so often produced spirited responses to vital issues.

Since this book was first published, many changes have taken place in the Borough. This is hardly surprising—there can be few towns in the land that have not experienced transition over the period of a quarter of a century. But not all the changes in Gosport have been to the advantage of the community. We have seen, for example, that in the eighteenth and nineteenth centuries, Gosport enjoyed the patronage of the armed forces, principally the Navy. This added colour and a certain pace to life as well as sustaining the local economy. That said, however, the town's relationship with the armed forces has always been an ambivalent one. A very large percentage of the Borough's acreage is still owned by the Ministry of Defence and, as we have seen, all too often this has worked against local plans. As John Arlott, writing in 'Hampshire' magazine in 1977, pointed out, "essentially the town is neither as rich nor as attractive as it might be because of the fundamental clash between the civic and service authorities." On the credit side, however, at least this has ensured that intensive development has not encroached upon some of the Borough's more sensitive areas. Stokes Bay and Gilkicker spring to mind here, both containing land still in Ministry of Defence ownership.

We have seen, too, that because of its peninsular configuration Gosport suffers from seemingly insoluble transport problems. Even in the 1920s, wise seers who observed the ominous development of the motor car were forecasting particular problems for Gosport if nothing was done. Perhaps it was unfortunate that Gosport should have gained a railway link to the outside world so early, for when the station was built the town still had its defence ramparts and the military insisted that the station was built outside the town. Perhaps if it had been in the town centre proper, the line would not have closed in the 1950s. As it

163

is, Gosport is one of the very few towns of its size in Britain without a railhead. This, together with the failure to retain the car ferry service and the abandonment of plans for a tunnel under the Harbour, must lead one to reflect upon neglected opportunities.

The development of huge, out-of-town shopping facilities has further isolated Gosport in recent years, while Fareham's large shopping complex has made the Gosport Town Centre Re-development Scheme—with a large supermarket as its centrepiece—an imperative. It is essential that both commerce and carefully planned housing are encouraged back into the town as we approach the year 2000.

Despite the example given by the handsome new library which was opened in 1973, the artistic and cultural life of the town has not flourished. In previous centuries, Gosport had two live theatres. Why none today? Other towns of comparative size manage to support small repertory theatres, and the interest in the town is there: witness the popularity of the hard-working local theatre and operatic societies. But the establishment of the Gosport Museum has been a success. Not only has it given a fillip to the study of local history, but also it has highlighted the varied artistic talents of local people in its regular exhibitions. In the superb paintings of Martin Snape we have a unique record of a Gosport long since vanished. A Snape Gallery with these eloquent testimonials of a bygone age as its centrepiece should be a major aim of the local authority, perhaps with financial help derived from business sponsorship.

What now of the future? Gosport is indisputably a harbour town, bound by ties of history and geography to Portsmouth. The current emphasis on 'Maritime Heritage' schemes would seem to be a pointer to the re-vitalization of the Borough's fortunes. Two major Ministry of Defence properties—St. George Barracks and Priddy's Hard—will shortly come into the public domain. Both buildings are part of our rich military heritage and their transfer to some form of community use will be watched with much interest. It is of major importance that the magnificent Powder Magazine at Priddy's Hard—with its eighteenth century harbour still intact—should remain as it is and not be split up to enrich other museum collections elsewhere in the country.

Gosport is still a fine place to live in. It has pleasant residential areas and its waterfront views are among the finest in the country. Our area is blessed with a mild climate—1987's hurricane notwithstanding!—and our sea air is fresh and unpolluted. Civic pride is a noble concept. Our future leaders must continue to plan for sensible growth in the Borough—to develop Gosport's leisure opportunities, to put pressure upon the service authorities to release land, to guard the open spaces and amenities for local people against faceless developers from outside. In the turbulent times which the future may bring, let us hope that they will remember that God's Port is Our Haven.

LIST OF MAYORS
OF THE BOROUGH SINCE INCORPORATION

1922–1924	J. F.Lee, J.P.
1924–1926	H. S. Masterman
1926–1927	W. G. Mogg, C.B.E.
1927–1930	B. A. Kent, J.P.
1930–1932	C. E. Davis
1932–1934	S. Barnard Smith
1934–1936	G. Ford
1936–1940	C. F. O. Graham, O.B.E.
1940–1946	J. R. Gregson, O.B.E., J.P.
1946–1949	A. R. Nobes, O.B.E., J.P.
1949–1953	C. B. Osborn
1953–1955	A. J. Eales, J.P.
1955–1957	H. T. Rogers, O.B.E.
1957–1959	P. D. Blanch
1959–1961	C. W. L. Giles
1961–1964	J. F. Fairhall
1964–1968	H. W. Cooley
1968–1970	V. E. J. Neal, M.B.E.
1970–1974	R. A. Kirkin
1974–1976	G. J. Hewitt
1976–1977	R. H. Borras, J.P.
1977–1978	T. R. Keith
1978–1979	Mrs F. B. Behrendt
1979–1980	R. A. Dimmer
1980–1981	D. D. Hope
1981–1982	G. S. Flory
1982–1983	Mrs A. Pearce
1983–1984	A. R. Williams
1984–1985	Mrs I. G. McBryde
1985–1986	D. J. Lucas
1986–1987	G. J. D. O'Neill
1987–1988	G. Rushton
1988–1989	Dr. H. A. B. Nicholls, M.A., M.R.C.G.P.

SOURCES AND BIBLIOGRAPHY

Historic Sketches of Gosport, Alverstoke and Rowner, by Arthur A. Walford (Walford & Sons, 1884)

Crossing the Harbour, by Lesley Burton & Brian Musselwhite (Ensign Publications, 1987)

The Earlier Fortifications of Gosport, by G. H. Williams (Gosport Society, 1974)

Gosport Goes to War, by Lesley Burton (Gosport Society, 1981)

Haslar—The Royal Hospital, by A. R. Revell (Gosport Society, 1978)

A History of Haslar Hospital, by William Tait (Griffin & Co., 1906)

Medicine and the Navy, Vol. III., by Lloyd & Coulter (Livingstone, 1978)

The Ancient and Modern History of Portsmouth, Portsea, Gosport and their Environs (J. Watts, 1901)

Illustrated History of Portsmouth, by W. G. Gates (Charpentier & Co., 1900)

The Annals of Portsmouth, by W. H. Saunders (Hamilton, Adams 1880)

Hampshire and the Isle of Wight, by Brian Vesey-Fitzgerald (Robert Hale, 1949)

The Western Defences of Portsmouth Harbour, 1400-1800, by G. H. Williams (Portsmouth Papers Series, Portsmouth City Council)

Arches of the Years, by Halliday Sutherland (G. Bles, 1933)

The Book of Snobs, by W. M. Thackeray (Appleton & Co., 1852)

Kelly's Directories, 1855-1976

White's Directory of Hampshire, 1878

Chamberlain's Complete History & Survey of London and Westminster, 1770

The Ecclesiastical History of the English Nation, by the Venerable Bede

The Anglo-Saxon Chronicles

Edition nos. 1-18 of the Gosport Records published by the Gosport Society

The Max Lock Report, 1948

The South Hampshire Structure Plan, 1971-4

Log books of Clarence Square Boys' School

"The Hampshire Telegraph"

"The Gosport Standard"

"The Hampshire Chronicle"

"The Evening News (later "The News")"

"Hampshire" magazine

CHAPTER 21

The Geology of Gosport

The Story of Gosport can be said to have begun with the formation of the ground on which the town is founded. Under a comparatively thin layer of topsoil, concrete or tarmac lie the clays, sands and gravels that form the foundation of the Borough.

The geological deposits were formed over a period of time ranging from about 50 million years ago to the present day in conditions that were very different to the Gosport that we know. For instance, some 40 to 50 million years ago, the area that is now southern England was submerged by shallow seas that gave way at times to estuaries and tidal flats. In these conditions, a sequence of sands and clays were deposited that now underlie the town and are encountered in excavations and foundation works.

The geological deposits of Gosport fall into two broad categories, based on their age of formation; those formed in the Tertiary period and those formed in Pleistocene and Holocene times.

The Tertiary period is defined as the time interval between about 60 million years ago and about 2.5 million years ago. Although this may seem a very considerable span of time, it needs to be borne in mind that current estimates of the age of the Earth are in the region of 4600 million years—so the Tertiary period represents a comparatively recent part of the geological past.

By the Tertiary period, the giant reptiles had already become extinct and the mammals were on the ascendant. In the area that is now southern England, the climate was warm, similar to sub-tropical climates today. Shallow seas covered much of the area to become southern England, although from time to time these gave way to other conditions. Figure 1 (see last illustration section) is an artist's impression of the area that was to become southern England, indicating the distribution of land and sea during the early part of the Tertiary period. All this was well before Man's appearance on the Earth, that occurred only some 1 to 2 million years ago.

During this Tertiary period, a sequence of sediments were deposited that now underlie Gosport. This sequence has been divided into a series of beds, formations and groups, based on the recognition of the obvious characteristics of the sediment and a comparison of the sequence with similar deposits elsewhere in southern England.

The delimitation of the extent of these formations etc. has been made by the British Geological Survey in the 1:63 360/1:50 000 scale geological map of the area. However, these maps are currently somewhat dated, having been geologically surveyed around the turn of the century. In the mid–1980s, the British Geological Survey remapped the area on a 1:10 000 scale but these maps and the accompanying report are not yet widely available. The geology of course has not changed since 1900 but much more information has come to light and ideas have evolved so today's interpretation of the distribution of the sub-surface deposits is somewhat different—in detail—to that made in 1900. Figure 2 is a simplified geological map based on the recent work of the British Geological Survey.

TERTIARY STRATA

Reading Formation

The Reading Formation (formerly known as the Reading Beds) is a sequence of predominantly red coloured mottled clays with some sandy layers. They occur at the base of the Tertiary sequence and (outside Gosport at the surface and beneath Gosport at depth) rest on top of the chalk. These clays, when unweathered, exhibit a tight network of natural joints—a feature known, in clays, as fissuring. This is an indication that the material has been subjected to burial (and subsequent unloading due to erosion) by the higher parts of the Tertiary sequence. Fissuring is rapidly obliterated once the clay is exposed at the surface, so the clay rapidly softens on exposure in excavations.

The clays of the Reading Formation were widely worked in south Hampshire for brick and tile making. The famous "Fareham Reds" were made from this clay, made at Funtley brickworks in Fareham.

In Gosport, the Reading Formation is present close to the surface adjacent to Fareham Creek where—at Foxbury Point there was formerly a brick and tile works. Unfortunately, good communications and the economies of scale have made local brickmaking uneconomic today. However, 100 years ago brickmaking (and not just from the Reading formation) was a significant local industry.

The Tertiary strata, although during deposition effectively horizontal, have been tilted to dip gently in a south-westerly direction. This tilting of the sequence occurred in the middle part of the Tertiary period, at approximately the same time as the main folding took place in the Alps. The tilted sequence was then eroded late in Tertiary times. The result is that the Tertiary strata now occur in approximately north-west to south-east trending outcrops with the Reading Formation at the north and the Bracklesham Group on the south side of the peninsula. Indeed it might be argued that the general orientation of the peninsula, in a north-west to south-east direction, is related to the trend of the underlying strata.

London Clay Formation

The London Clay Formation (informally known as the London Clay) overlies the Reading Formation and occupies the northern part of the peninsula. The term "clay" in the title is rather misleading however; although much of the formation is a fissured grey clay (which on weathering becomes brown), thick beds of compacted sand also occur. A prominent bed of sand occurs near the top of the formation: this sand bed was formerly referred to as the "Bagshot Sands" and considered a separate geological formation. Modern usage however considers this sand to be part of the London Clay Formation, and it is referred to as the Whitecliff Sand member of that formation. The clays of the London Clay Formation are often highly fossiliferous and typical fossils are shown in Figure 3. Little is seen of the formation at the surface, although intermittent exposures occur along the shore of Portsmouth Harbour (see King and Kemp 1980).

Bracklesham Group

Much of the central and southern part of the peninsula is underlain by a very varied sequence of clays, clayey sands and sands known as the Bracklesham Group (formerly referred to as the Bracklesham Beds). The varied nature of this sequence is highlighted by its "group" status. Within the Group, four separate formations have now been recognised, the Wittering Formation, the Earnsley Sand Formation, the Marsh Farm Formation and the Selsey Sand Formation.

The clayey sands often have in their unweathered form a greenish hue but on exposure weather yellow-brown. In the Bracklesham Group, interbedded sands and clay occur such that the layers are millimetres in thickness; this laminated material characteristically occurs in the Wittering Formation of the Bracklesham Group.

In addition, a dark brown or black "coaly" material is associated with the Bracklesham group. This is lignite and represents plant material incorporated in the sediment at the time of deposition.

The Bracklesham Group is, in places, highly fossiliferous and well exposed at low tide at Lee-on-the-Solent (see Kemp 1985). Here an excellent and varied selection of fossils may be collected (see Figure 4). The group is widely encountered, however, in shallow excavations and foundations inland as is indicated by the distribution of the group on the geological map.

The presence of rapidly softening clays of the Bracklesham group at Lee made the construction of the sea wall difficult, but before the construction of these works, fossils from the Bracklesham Group could be found in the cliff.

PLEISTOCENE AND HOLOCENE DEPOSITS

The strata described above were formed in the early part of the Tertiary period known as the Eocene epoch. Tilting of the sequence took place in the middle of Tertiary times (about 25 million years ago). On top of these tilted and eroded Tertiary strata were deposited a variable sequence of Pleistocene and Holocene deposits over much of the area that is now Gosport. These deposits are sometimes referred to as "Drift" or as "Superficial Deposits"—the latter term being highly misleading, since these deposits may be many metres in thickness.

The Pleistocene period succeeds the Tertiary period and is deemed to have started 2.5 million years ago and finished 10,000 years ago. The Holocene period succeeds the Pleistocene and thus began 10,000 years ago and is still continuing! The Pleistocene and Holocene are sometimes referred to together as the Quaternary while some geologists refer to the Holocene as the Flandrian.

During the later part of the Tertiary period, the climate became markedly cooler and in the Pleistocene much larger areas of the northern hemisphere were covered with ice sheets than at present. This Pleistocene glaciation was not continuous, however, but a period of major ice advances and retreats; some of the interglacial episodes, between the ice advances, were warmer than our present climate! It was during the Pleistocene period that Man developed into our modern form. The archaeological ages occurred in Europe during the later part of the Pleistocene and the Holocene.

It is believed, on the basis of the deposits found in the area, that southern England escaped thick ice cover although the ground would have undergone disturbance by freezing and thawing in the zone that was peripheral to the ice sheet. This was the periglacial zone.

Pleistocene Gravels

Over much of Gosport, gravels up to several metres in thickness overlie the Tertiary strata. These gravels consist, usually, of sub-angular to sub-rounded flint fragments with subordinate amounts of sand and clay. Currently, these gravels are being quarried at Lee, close to the River Alver. In past times, gravel digging was much more widespread in Gosport with pits in the Clayhall area supplying thousands of tons of gravel for railway ballast.

The Pleistocene gravels are believed to represent the terrace deposits of an easterly flowing "Solent River" that was present during the Pleistocene. Formerly they were mapped by the British Geological Survey as "Plateau Gravel" and "Valley Gravel" but this terminology is now considered obsolete.

Brickearth

Brickearth is a relatively homogeneous yellow-brown compact silt deposit of Pleistocene age that—as the name implies—was widely used for brickmaking (although, as we have seen, it was not the only brickmaking material to occur in the Borough). Brickearth was known locally as "pug" and it occurs as a layer, up to 1½ metres in thickness, capping either the Pleistocene gravels or resting directly on the Tertiary strata.

Much of the central part of the peninsula, between Stoke Road and Forton Road is underlain by Brickearth much of which has been won for brickmaking. Because the Brickearth is a comparatively thin deposit, the workings needed to be laterally extensive to win the required quantities of the material, thus the workings were brickfields rather than brickpits. Such brickfields were widespread in Gosport especially when building materials were required for the expansion of the town in the 19th Century. Leesland is an area where extensive brickfields were in existence; the Moreland allotments being the site of a brickfield. Elsewhere, after the Brickearth had been won, building took place on the new, lower, surface exposed by the winning operation.

Alluvium

The term Alluvium is applied to deposits of sand, silt and clay that have accumulated in the late Pleistocene and Holocene periods. These are the soft "muds" often with a high organic content i.e. they have an undesirable odour. Alluvium represents the deposits of rivers and streams and may be in some circumstances, many metres in thickness. Peaty material may occur as part of these deposits.

Such alluvial deposits underlie Portsmouth Harbour and the other tidal inlets of the town. Alluvium also occurs underlying the valley of the Alver. The low lying marshy ground close to the sea near Bay House School is underlain by thick alluvial deposits. Alluvial deposits are also found associated with the low ground to the south of St. Mary's Church in Alverstoke and with the former mill pond (Mill Lane) in Forton.

Alluvial deposits are, of course, still being formed in and around Gosport as part of the continuing geological development of the area, geological processes may be slightly modified by Man but never eliminated.

G. R. J. Browning
M.Sc(Lond), D.I.C., C.Eng., FIMM., FGS.
Member, Institution of Geologists.

References:

King, C. & Kemp, D. J. 1980 Exposures in the London Clay Formation of the Gosport Area. *Hampshire Tertiary Research 3(2):71-81*

Kemp, D. J., King, A. D., 1979 Stratigraphy and Biota of the King, C., & Quayle, W. J. Elmore Formation (Hunting-bridge Division, Bracklesham Group) at Lee-on-the-Solent, Gosport, Hants. *Hampshire Tertiary Research 2(2)*

Kemp, D. J. 1985 The Selsey Division (Bracklesham Group) at Lee-on-the-Solent, Gosport, Hants. *Hampshire Tertiary Research 7(2):35-44*

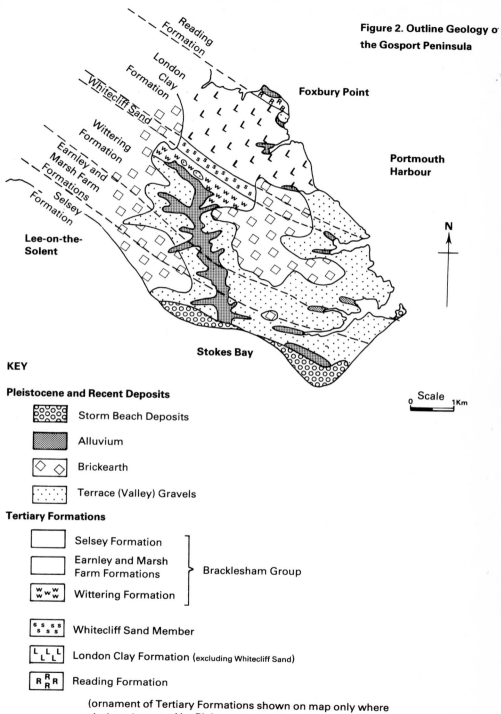

Figure 2. Outline Geology o the Gosport Peninsula

Foxbury Point

Portmouth Harbour

N

Lee-on-the-Solent

Stokes Bay

KEY

Pleistocene and Recent Deposits

- Storm Beach Deposits
- Alluvium
- Brickearth
- Terrace (Valley) Gravels

Tertiary Formations

- Selsey Formation
- Earnley and Marsh Farm Formations ⎫ Bracklesham Group
- w w w / w w w Wittering Formation ⎭
- s s s s / s s s Whitecliff Sand Member
- L L L / L L London Clay Formation (excluding Whitecliff Sand)
- R R R / R Reading Formation

(ornament of Tertiary Formations shown on map only where strata not covered by Pleistocene and Recent Deposits)

Scale
0 ___ 1Km

173

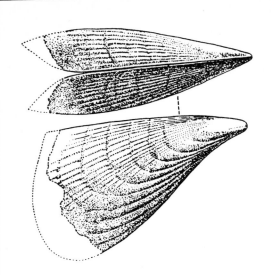

Pinna affinis J. Sowerby. (×½.)

Turritella imbricataria Lamarck.(×1.)

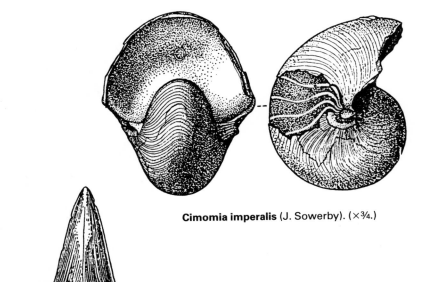

Cimomia imperalis (J. Sowerby). (×¾.)

FIGURE 3.

FOSSILS FROM THE
LONDON CLAY FORMATION

Otodus obliquus Agassiz. (×1.)

FIGURE 4.

FOSSILS FROM THE BRACKLESHAM GROUP

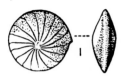

Nummulites variolarius Lamarck. (×15)

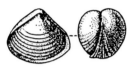

Corbula pisum J. Sowerby. (×3.)

Protula extensa Solander. (×1.)

Campanile cornucopiae J. Sowerby. (×½.)

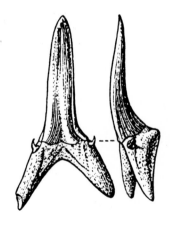

Eugomphodus macrotus Agassiz. (×1½.)

175

FIGURE 4
continued

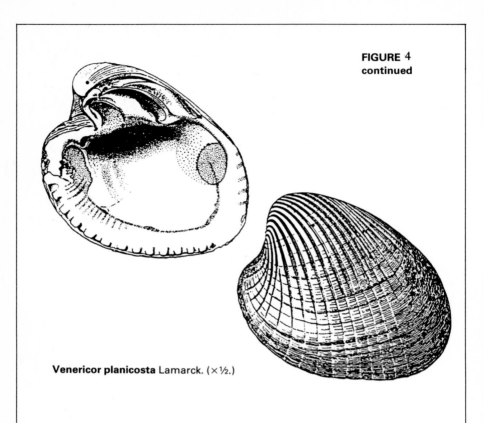

Venericor planicosta Lamarck. (×½.)

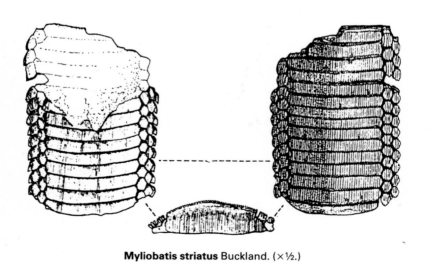

Myliobatis striatus Buckland. (×½.)